# MARCO ⊕ POLO

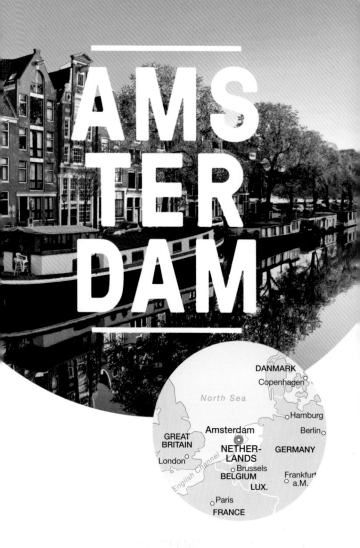

# AMS TER DAM

**DANMARK**
Copenhagen

*North Sea*

Hamburg

Amsterdam

Berlin

**GREAT BRITAIN**
London

**NETHER-LANDS**

**GERMANY**

Brussels
**BELGIUM**

Frankfurt a.M.

**LUX.**

Paris
**FRANCE**

*English Channel*

**FREE!**

# THE
# TOURING APP

shows you the way...

including routes and offline maps!

# GET MORE OUT OF YOUR MARCO POLO GUIDE

IT'S AS SIMPLE AS THIS

**1** go.marco-polo.com/ams

**2** download and discover

# GO!

WORKS OFFLINE!

**SYMBOLS**

| INSIDER TIP | Insider Tip |
| ★ | Highlight |
| ⬤⬤⬤⬤ | Best of... |
| ☆ | Scenic view |
| ⊘ | Responsible travel: for ecological or fair trade aspects |
| (*) | Telephone numbers that are not toll-free |

**PRICE CATEGORIES HOTELS**

| *Expensive* | over 180 euros |
| *Moderate* | 120–180 euros |
| *Budget* | under 120 euros |

Prices are for one night for a double room with breakfast

**PRICE CATEGORIES RESTAURANTS**

| *Expensive* | over 45 euros |
| *Moderate* | 30–45 euros |
| *Budget* | under 30 euros |

Prices for a meal with starter, main course and dessert, without drinks

---

**DID YOU KNOW?**
Curtain up! → p. 25
Time to chill → p. 32
The starship has landed → p. 40
Fit in the City → p. 43
Immigrants in the park → p. 53
Local specialities → p. 60
Favourite eateries → p. 62
For bookworms and film buffs → p. 82
More than a good night's sleep → p. 88

**MAPS IN THE GUIDEBOOK**
(128 A1) Page numbers and coordinates refer to the street atlas and the map of Amsterdam and surrounding area on p. 138/139
(0) Site/address located off the map
Coordinates are also given for places that are not marked on the street atlas.

(🕮 A–B 2–3) refers to the removable pull-out map

**INSIDE FRONT COVER:**
The best highlights

**INSIDE BACK COVER:**
Tram, railway and underground route map

# The best MARCO POLO Insider Tips

## Our top 15 Insider Tips

**INSIDER TIP** **Hot and crispy**
The *prawn croquettes* from *Holtkamp bakery* are a city-wide speciality → **p. 25**

**INSIDER TIP** **Where it's happening**
Built as a workers' quarter, today *De Pijp* is characterised by its intriguing, colourful mix of student pubs, chic restaurants, market bustle and Asian shops → **p. 49**

**INSIDER TIP** **Picturesque dyke village**
*Nieuwendam* offers country flair in the city. Although it is now part of Amsterdam, it has kept its village atmosphere with old wooden houses → **p. 54**

**INSIDER TIP** **The glory of handbags**
The large collection of the *Hendrikje Museum of Bags and Purses* dates from the Middle Ages up to the present. It is simply a must for fashionistas → **p. 43**

**INSIDER TIP** **17th-century hang out**
*Café Hoppe* first opened in 1670 and has hardly changed ever since. In the afternoon (after 5 pm), half of Amsterdam seems to gather in front of this pub on the Spui → **p. 36**

**INSIDER TIP** **Say cheese**
*Kaashuis Tromp* lives up to all the clichés: all sorts of cheeses are piled up to the ceiling in this little shop → **p. 70**

**INSIDER TIP** **Unexpected flavours**
*Puccini's* hand-made chocolates release their very own, surprising flavours with ingredients like nutmeg, pepper and gin (photo above) → **p. 71**

**INSIDER TIP** **A secret church in the attic**
This canal house lives up to its name, 'our dear Lord in the attic'. A *secret church* is hidden under its eaves → **p. 36**

**INSIDER TIP Futuristic footwear**
The footwear from *United Nude* is said to reflect the designer's connection to the famous architect Rem Koolhaas. With their creative heels, these shoes are coveted around the world → **p. 74**

**INSIDER TIP Green cuisine**
*De Kas* serves up modern Dutch organic cuisine with ingredients from its own garden in an old eight-metre high greenhouse → **p. 61**

**INSIDER TIP A piece of cake**
All of Amsterdam is raving about the traditional Dutch apple pie called *appeltaart* at *Winkel 43*. People queue up for ages just to get a slice → **p. 58**

**INSIDER TIP Open-air museum**
*A showcase of contemporary architecture* ranging from experimental residential buildings to the iconic film museum can be found along the banks of the IJ → **p. 106**

**INSIDER TIP Bobbing bungalows**
Amsterdam's *houseboats* are certainly pretty to look at. But if you really want to experience life on the water, with all the splashing, rocking and bobbing up and down, then book one for a night. Or two or three... (photo below) → **p. 85**

**INSIDER TIP Eating on the go**
Although streetfood was once very much an Asian thing, it has become a European trend of late. The *dozens of stands* in an old tram depot on the western side of town are on a mission to breathe new life into the food scene → **p. 58**

**INSIDER TIP Design in your room**
A hostel in which a shipping line once housed emigrants bound for life overseas has now made way for art and design. The individually styled rooms of the magnificent *Lloyd Hotel* guarantee an unconventional overnight stay → **p. 89**

# BEST OF...

**FOR FREE**

● *Film after film*

In the basement of the *Eye Film Institute*, you can cuddle up and watch films from the collection in a viewing pod built for two – even for hours on end, if you want → p. 53

● *Park life*

Amsterdam's place to meet in summer is *Vondelpark*. Listen to one of the many free open-air concerts, have a picnic or play football. This park is a magnet for social gatherings rather than a place for peace and quiet (photo) → p. 52, 80

● *Midday classics*

The lunchtime concerts in the *Concertgebouw* are an Amsterdam institution – and they are free. Every Wednesday at 12:30 pm you can enjoy a rehearsal of the Concertgebouw Orchestra or listen to a half-hour concert by talented young musicians → p. 49

● *Open-air cinema*

The *Pluk de Nacht* outdoor film festival held on a small peninsula on Westerdoksdijk runs over several weeks in August. You only have to pay if you want a warm blanket to go with your deckchair → p. 113

● *Galleries in Jordaan*

If you want to catch up on contemporary art, you don't always have to buy a ticket. The alternative is a wander through the art galleries on the streets of Amsterdam. Most of the renowned galleries, for example *Fons Welters, Annet Gelink* or *Torch,* are situated close together in the Jordaan district → p. 38, 71

● *As colourful as it gets*

The Chinese like things to be colourful. Among the old brick buildings on Zeedijk stands the Buddhist *Fo Guang Shan He Hua Temple,* where you can catch a glimpse of the religious heart of Amsterdam's Chinatown → p. 33

◖◗◖◗◖◗ Dots in guidebook refer to "Best of..." tips

# ONLY IN AMSTERDAM
## Unique experiences

● *Cycle city*

You can't imagine Amsterdam without bicycles. Thanks to many hire stations, visitors can pedal around just as the locals do. At *Star Bikes Rental* the service is extremely friendly, and they make a good latte macchiato → p. 116

● *Life on the canal*

The houses on Amsterdam's canals (canal = "gracht") can be crooked and leaning to one side, or imposing and elegant. Lining the canals of the old part of town, shoulder to shoulder, they are all built of brick, but when you look more closely, no two are alike. The finest residences are in the *Gouden Bocht* (Golden Arc) on Herengracht → p. 40

● *Brown cafés*

With wood-panelling all around, the "brown cafés" that you find on almost every corner in Amsterdam are without a doubt cosy and sociable. Some examples of this type of establishment, like *De Oosterling* or *Wynand Fockink,* are several hundred years old → p. 78, 79

● *Royal date*

Since Queen Beatrix's abdication in 2013, the former Koninginnedag has become *Koningsdag.* On this day, the 27th April, everyone in the Netherlands celebrates their King Willem-Alexander. The day begins with a city-wide flea market which then turns into a street party towards the afternoon. This is not only an opportunity to get dressed in orange from head to toe but also to take to the canals → p. 112

● *Bridges everywhere*

In the historic parts of the city there are no less than 600 bridges, the most famous of which is the *Magere Brug* across the Amstel. At the junction of Reguliersgracht and Herengracht you can even take in 15 bridges all at once → p. 42

● *All around the globe*

Sometimes the shelves are filled with foodstuffs from Thailand, Surinam and India, and salsa music pours out of the stereo in the background. If you want to see how cosmopolitan Amsterdam is, peek inside one of the *tokos,* the little shops that sell exotic provisions, for example around Albert Cuypmarkt → p. 69

ONLY IN

# BEST OF...

● *A new kind of library*
In the public *Openbare Bibliotheek* you can do more than just read books. Take a walk around, admire the furnishings made by Dutch designers, surf the internet for free, listen to music, leaf through international newspapers or have a coffee → p. 32

● *Underwater worlds*
A zoo is not the obvious place to go in bad weather, but *Artis* is different. This historic aquarium shows you life under the seas, and there is also a butterfly pavilion with colourful specimens → p. 110

● *Cosy cinema*
*The Movies* on Haarlemmerdijk is Amsterdam's oldest cinema and has retained its Art Deco styling. After the film, stay for a beer in the cosy cinema pub → p. 82

● *Shopping in the post office*
The *Magna Plaza* shopping centre was built in the late 19th century as the main post office. Today this imposing Gothic Revival building houses upmarket fashion stores and cafés situated around its spacious courtyards → p. 68

● *A trip overseas*
The *Tropenmuseum* brings to life the colonial past of the Netherlands and also conveys an impression of life in far-away countries today – including a storm in the African savannah and a boat trip through the rainforest (photo) → p. 48

● *From the city hall to the palace*
King Willem-Alexander rarely stays in the *Koninklijk Paleis*, which was originally built as a city hall. All the same, its impressive rooms are well worth seeing – especially the Great Hall, which depicts the universe with Amsterdam at its centre → p. 33

RAIN

# RELAX AND CHILL OUT
## Take it easy and spoil yourself

● *Art Deco sauna*
The *Sauna Déco* lies right on Herengracht. This 600 m² (6,458 sq. ft.) sauna complex has been furnished with the Art Deco interior of a Paris department store that was demolished. The lead glass windows and ornamental lamps make it a particularly good place to relax → **p. 32**

● *Hippy paradise*
*Blijburg aan Zee,* on the eastern edge of the newly built IJburg quarter, is an oasis for hippies. In summer abandon yourself to the lazy pleasures of sunshine and water on this nicely improvised city beach → **p. 54**

● *Just swim*
Amsterdam's most attractive swimming pool, the *Zuiderbad,* has little to offer apart from a single pool in a historic building. But that is exactly what makes it so relaxing: you can come here simply to swim in peace → **p. 46**

● *A spa on the forest's edge*
Zuiver" is the Dutch word for "clean", and a stay at the *Hotel Spa Zuiver* is guaranteed to make you just that. On the edge of the Amsterdamse Bos woodland, it offers a spa holiday in the south of the city – with or without an overnight stay → **p. 90**

● *A café with atmosphere*
The *NEMO* in the Oosterdok (photo) looks like a beached whale. You can walk up the terraced back of the building, and in summer there is an open-air café at the top with beanbags for seats and a fantastic view across historic Amsterdam. Parents can sip a glass of rosé while their children play in the paddling pool → **p. 111**

● *Hire a boat*
Rather than jumping aboard a tour, glide leisurely through the canals of Amsterdam at your own pace in a small hired *fluisterboot* ("whisper boat"). A licence is not required for these electric boats → **p. 117**

INTRODUCTION

# DISCOVER AMSTERDAM!

The *narrow houses* lean on each other at a slight angle. A *cyclist* crosses a bridge on his squeaking bike, and outside the café on the corner, people sit in the sun enjoying a beer. In the distance you can hear a tram rumbling across Leidseplein. There is no doubt that Amsterdam is a beautiful city. It charms millions of visitors every year with its relaxed and yet lively atmosphere. Just about everyone feels right at home surrounded by the old houses and pretty bridges on the canals. The secret of its success lies in the fact that Amsterdam is an *incredibly diverse* city, despite the fact that it is most likely the smallest metropolis in the world. Old and new, calm and bustling, artistic and commercial, provincial and cosmopolitan – there is no way to describe the city of canals without such contradictions. With almost *8500 listed buildings,* Amsterdam boasts the highest density of historic monuments in the Netherlands. The historic *Canal Ring* has been an Unesco World Heritage site since 2010. In the old core of the city there is a piece of Dutch history to discover on each and every corner, from *carved gable stones* to old shipyards and a *secret church* below the roof of a canalside house.

Photo: Dutch-style canal houses on the Herengracht

As its centre is compact, Amsterdam, which is built on *90 islands,* is a wonderful city for strolling about. Only by walking along the brick-paved streets by the *canals* can you take in the elegance of the tall, narrow-fronted burghers' houses, spot the heron on the roof of a *houseboat,* or discover here and there a hidden *hofje* (courtyard) or a little antique shop. The historic ensemble of the Canal Ring has been preserved in its entirety over centuries. For this reason the whole city centre was listed as a historic site in 1999. And in other districts too, for example in *Jordaan* with its village-like character, time seems to have stood still. The fact that Amsterdam is not some lifeless open-air museum but rather a vibrant city has something to do with the *relaxed* attitude of the Dutch when it comes to their historic buildings – as in the case of neon signs on a Gothic stepped gable – but it also stems in part from the city's exceptionally cosmopolitan and *young population.* Half of Amsterdam residents do not come from the Netherlands, and 41 per cent of them are under 35 years of age. This is what gives the *nightlife* around Leidseplein and Rembrandtplein such a *buzz.* It also accounts for the almost unlimited range of shopping options in the city as well as the abundance of cafés, bars and restaurants that make it hard to decide where to go.

> **Almost half the population is under 35 years of age**

Amsterdam is appealing at any time of the year – in summer, when the cafés put tables out on the street and an almost *Mediterranean atmosphere* prevails, or in winter,

Whether historic or modern, Amsterdam's architecture is impressive

when the canals are veiled in mist and the *bridges* sport twinkling lights. Its main attractions include three major museums, the Rijksmuseum, Van Gogh Museum and Stedelijk Museum with their unique *art treasures,* and the numerous little shops, *winkels,* in the city centre. And, last but not least, the popularity of Amsterdam as a destination for visitors from all over the world has to do with the open and good-natured character of its people.

The mentality of the Amsterdammers with their commercial spirit and proverbial tolerance has had a decisive influence on the history of the Dutch capital. The city originated as a marshy *fishing village* at the point where the river *Amstel* flowed into the *IJsselmeer,* which is now a lake but was then part of the North Sea. In 1275 the village of Amstelledamme was granted *freedom from customs duties* and a town charter followed in 1300. From then onwards, thanks to its location, the town controlled the flow of goods between the North Sea and the Dutch hinterland. The commercially-minded Amsterdammers were always on the lookout for new

> **A commercial spirit and proverbial tolerance**

opportunities: it was not long before they were *trading* with the whole of the Baltic Sea and the North Sea regions. To protect themselves against high tides, they started to construct a line of defences, de *wallen.* The oldest quarter of the city between Oudezijds and Nieuwezijds Achterburgwal, which has been well preserved for the most part, is now *Chinatown* and the *red light district.*

At the end of the 16th century the northern Netherlands gained independence from Spanish rule in the 80 Years War. In this period Amsterdam gained an early reputation for being liberal, which attracted many Protestant and Jewish refugees from places like Antwerp and Lisbon that were still ruled by Spain. The influx of wealthy merchants among these *immigrants* extended trade connections and ushered in the so-called *Golden Age.* In 1602 the Dutch East India Company *(Verenigde Oostindische Compagnie, VOC)* was established with a monopoly of *maritime trade* with the Far East and India, and in 1621 the Westindische Compagnie was founded to carry out trade with America and the west coast of Africa. Over the following 150 years, the Netherlands became one of the leading European naval and commercial powers. Amsterdam grew to be a *rich and important port* with warehouses full of cloves, cinnamon, silk, coffee and porcelain. Within a few decades, the number of residents increased five-fold.

In the early 17th century, with the city bursting at the seams, construction was started on the concentric rings of canals. Outside the old *wallen*, rich merchants built *fine residences* with attached warehouses on Herengracht, Keizersgracht or Prinsengracht. And these impressive domiciles naturally had to be outfitted with pretty things, heralding in the *glory days* of Dutch art. The greatest works of the Golden Age such as Rembrandt's *Nightwatch* and Vermeer's *Kitchen Maid* can be admired in the *Rijksmuseum* today – a reminder of a time in which gold not only disappeared into the pockets of the rich, but also fed the talent of artists, who then had the means to create such masterpieces.

Around 1700 Amsterdam boasted a population of about 220,000 inhabitants, which made it the third-largest city in Europe, and it had reached the peak of its prosperity. Just fifty years later, the glory of the Netherlands had begun to fade as other countries took over the rule of the seas. The economy began to recover in the mid-19th century thanks to *industrialisation* and the construction of the *Nordzeekanal,* which enabled ocean-going ships to enter the port of Amsterdam.

During *World War II,* the Netherlands fell to German forces after five days of fighting. The speed of the capitulation meant that Amsterdam suffered little damage, preserving the city's historic architecture. A strong *resistance* movement to the German occupation formed, but it was not able to prevent the almost complete annihilation of the city's Jewish community, including Anne Frank, the country's most well-known Holocaust victim.

> **Coffee shops and gay marriage give the city a certain image**

In the 1970s Amsterdam became a colourful mecca for *hippies, squatters* and *drop-outs* from all over the world. Although it is hard to imagine today, thousands of backpackers camped out in Vondelpark and on the Dam in summer, and by 1980 the population of the city included some 20,000 squatters. Liberal politicians brought about the *legalisation* of soft *drugs,* and every marginal group was free to do its own thing. This reputation still clings to Amsterdam even today – not just tulips and canals, but also "coffee shops" and the red light district are part of the city's image.

A few years ago, however, the general mentality began to change, and the Dutch have become noticeably *more conservative*. Squatting has been illegal since the end of 2010, and coffee shops in the border provinces are only permitted to cater to customers with Dutch residence passes. But Amsterdam still dances to its own tune. Despite the growing criticism in the canal city towards the *ineffective integration* and *high unemployment rates* among the Moroccan and Turkish immigrant populations, the city council still leans to the Left, and coffee shops are open to everyone. The *prohibition on squatting* has been enforced, however, so that occupied houses, known as *kraakpand* and once a familiar sight all over he city, are becoming increasingly rare. By way of contrast, *cranes* and *building ites* have become more and more common. A lot has happened in recent years, specially on the banks of the IJ. Whereas completely *new quarters* of the city ave risen up in the former dockland area to the east of the main station, construction work around the new *Eye Film Institute* on the north bank and in the old imber docks to the west of the inner city is still in progress. The Amsterdammers re not fans of letting things settle, though, which is why the hot spots of city life re moving out of the city centre into the former residential and shipping districts on its outskirts.

n the historic centre, much of this still goes unnoticed. Amsterdam is and will remain a compact, remarkably aid-back, sometimes rather chaotic metropolis with about *812,000 inhabitants.* The Amsterdammers' preferred

**Compact, remarkably laid-back, sometimes chaotic**

means of transport is still the eco-friendly *fiets* (bicycle), usually rusty. On summer weekends, residents love to chug along the canals in little *boats* drinking a glass of rosé, or sit in the sun with a cup of coffee on the pavement in front of their houses. *Cafés* are an important part of life in the city. Whether dark pubs, cool design bars or candle-lit snugs – what matters is that they are *gezellig,* cosy and sociable.

Thanks to its enormous diversity, Amsterdam attracts many different kinds of visitors. But when the elms are reflected in the water of the canals and the glockenspiel of the Westerkerk chimes in the background, they are all equally fascinated.

Amsterdam's "gezellig" atmosphere can even be felt outdoors in places such as the former NDSM shipyard

# WHAT'S HOT

## 1 Home cooking

*Private dining* Chefs invite you into their own homes and serve a meal on grandmother's dinner service. Home cooking is all the rage in Amsterdam. One of the foremost exponents is Marit Beemster with her *Eetkamer (Andreas Bonnstraat 34h | www.maritseetkamer.nl)*. Adrienne Eisma also invites guests to her home *(The Cookery | Valeriusstraat 250 | www.thecookery.nl)*. On the north shore of the IJ, Tinda van Smorenburg cooks up seasonal dishes at her *IJ-Keuken (Koperslagerij 51 | www.ij-keuken.nl)*.

## 2 Fresh off the press

*Art* Canal houses made of brick and timber are a familiar sight. But, architecture has now gone high-tech. Amsterdam is going to be the home of the first *3D printed canal house (Asterweg 49 | 3dprintcanalhouse.com) (photo)*. *DUS Architects* have developed a huge 3D printer to create a house made of 🌀 bio-based plastic granulate piece by piece. A visitors' centre was opened in early 2017 that documents the story of the house's design and construction.

## 3 Spot on

*Trendy quarter* The lure of the filthy: an increasing number of restaurant and café owners are rediscovering the red light district *(photo)*. Among the new establishments that are nestled between sex shops and windows of prostitutes are the cosy café and restaurant *Mata Hari (Oudezijds Achterburgwal 22 | www.matahari-amsterdam.nl)*, the *Metropolitan Deli (Warmoesstraat 111 | www.metropolitandeli.nl)* and the renowned *Restaurant Anna (Warmoesstraat 111 | www.restaurantanna.nl)*.

## There are lots of new things to discover in Amsterdam. A few of the most interesting are listed below

# Bench Days

4

***Friendly neighbours*** Anyone who has walked around the canal rings on a sunny Friday afternoon has undoubtedly spotted the locals sitting in front of their houses with a glass of wine and a newspaper, or chatting with their neighbours. This tradition has been turned into an event by the *Bankjescollectief (www.bankjescollectief.nl) (photo)*. It sponsors so-called "Bench Days" across the city on different days, where you can take a seat and enjoy a warm mug of hot cocoa or a glass of white wine (depending on the time of year) with local residents. This initiative is an international success story, and "bench days" are popping up all over, but they're still most popular in the Netherlands.

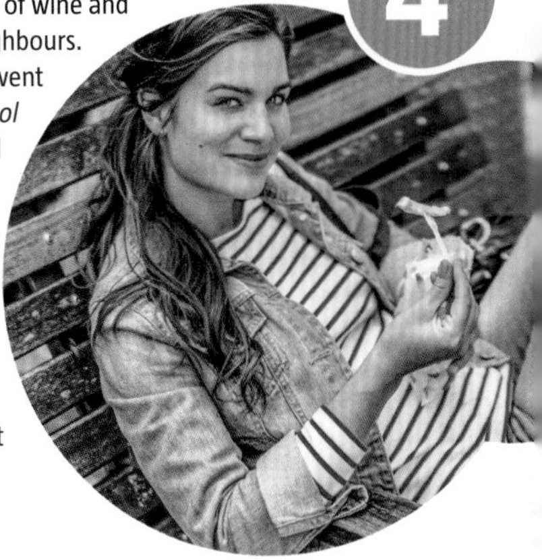

# Body and soul

5

***Paddle, float, climb*** Standup paddleboarding is an almost meditative experience. If you don't know the ropes, take part in one of the courses offered by *M & M SUP (www.mm-sup.com) (photo)* on the IJburg. In the summer months they also organise paddling sessions by night, *Night SUP*. If that's not enough to calm you down, try floating. Drifting in the weightless saltwater pool of *Koan Float* is a great antidote to stress *(Herengracht 321 | www.koanfloat.nl)*. One of the winter attractions is the *Jaap Eden* indoor ice rink *(Radioweg 64 | www.jaapeden.nl)* in the suburb of Watergraafsmeer. The Amsterdammers glide with elegance and endurance around the rink, aided by the long upward curving speed skates that are standard in the Netherlands. If you want to try them out, you can rent them *(an ID or a deposit of 100 euros is necessary)*.

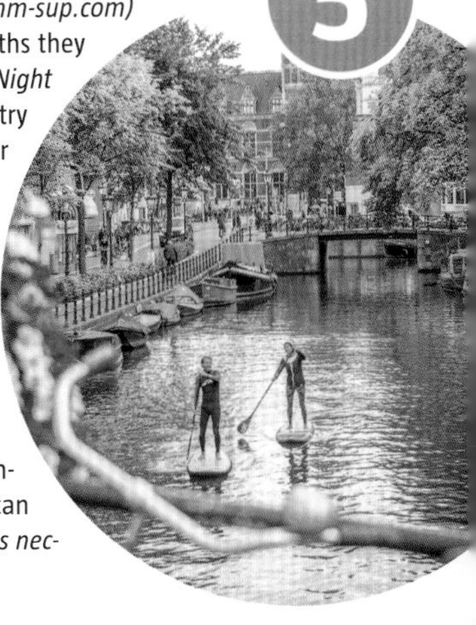

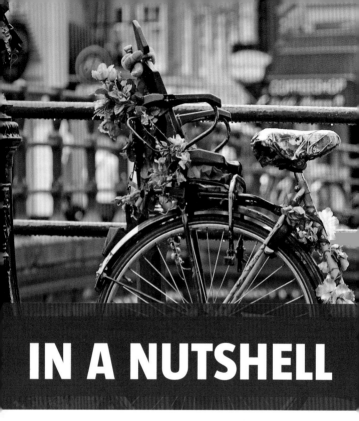

# IN A NUTSHELL

## FIETSEN, FIETSEN, FIETSEN

There are said to be more than 880,000 bicycles in Amsterdam, which is more than the city's population. Around one third of the locals always travel by bike – in a compact but permanently congested city with few parking spaces, a *fiets* is the best way to go. Cyclists are allowed to do almost anything, such as riding side by side and transporting passengers on the carrier rack. For some years now there has been a focus on bike lights. The authorities regularly check cyclists' lights in the evenings. Most bikes in the city are in an awful condition. This is deliberate because if a bike looks too expensive, it will be stolen in next to no time.

## OPEN THE LOCKS

Amsterdam is known as the "Venice of the north". This nickname comes from the many *grachten*, or canals, that are the hallmark of the historic city centre. The canals once functioned as sewers. Once a day, the sluice gates were opened and the dirty water flowed out into the Zuiderzee, now called the IJsselmeer. Nowadays the water is still circulated several times a week. In the 1960s and 1970s several canals were filled in for the sake of road traffic in the historic centre. Only their names – Vijzelgracht, Lindengracht, Palmgracht – serve as a reminder that these streets were once waterways.

Houseboats, royals and snacks:
What's characteristic, remarkable and
peculiar in the city of canals

## S EMI-LEGAL GRASS

The Netherlands is the only country in the world where the public sale of up to 5 grams of cannabis is tolerated. The sale of cannabis is illegal, but it is just not prosecuted. This contradiction works according to the principle of *gedogen,* which translates as tolerance. This policy is intended to draw a line between the markets for hard and soft drugs. Yet this approach is not without its problems, especially since the coffee shop owners operate in a kind of grey zone because they sell wares that are illegal to grow or import into the country. How are they supposed to get a hold of cannabis without relying on a black market? The city has done its best to clamp down on the coffee shops by tightening regulations. These measures have been somewhat successful in reducing the number of coffee shops from about 300 in 1999 to only 200 or so today.

But, as the saying goes, seek and you will (still ) find…

# DUTCH DESIGN

All over the world, products by Dutch designers, generally simple but quirky, are much sought after. It all started with *Droog Design* (literally: dry design), a collective of young designers who got together in the mid-1990s in Amsterdam to develop an alternative to the super-smooth, high-gloss side of the design world. In no time at all, their first products – including an armchair made from old clothing bundled together and a chandelier from a bunch of light bulbs – were world-famous.

In the meantime, Dutch design has almost become a brand, and Droog Design has opened a popular store-cum-gallery in Staalstraat, where unusual products by young designers are on sale. The most internationally successful former Droog designer, Marcel Wanders, is now taking a different path: he has opted for the fanciful forms of neo-Baroque, but does so with tongue in cheek. Since 2009, an old school in Jordaan has been home to his design label *Moooi*. He got the opportunity to move in here thanks to the city council of Amsterdam, which has consciously supported the design business in recent years. The city also sponsored the furnishing of the public library with Dutch designer pieces and has promoted the establishment of young designers in the red light district where studios have been set up in former brothels. These endeavours speak volumes about the way Amsterdam would like to develop as a tourist destination.

# MAYOR(S) OF THE CITY

Every city needs a mayor, but not every city has three! While the city of canals only has one proper mayor, it also has as a night-mayor and a bicycle-mayor. The night-mayor represents the interests of Amsterdam's nightlife, serving as a mediator between the city, the residents and the entertainment industry. In 2014, he pushed through permission for some clubs to operate around the clock. The office of the bicycle-mayor was created in 2016, and it has been occupied by Anna Luten, the "voice of cyclists at city hall". Her job is to take care of improving the city's bike paths and parking options while advocating for the interests of cyclists (although some visitors might not think this is really necessary in Amsterdam…).

# HET IJ

A large stretch of water behind the main station, the *IJ* (pronounced something like "eye"), forms the northern border of the inner city of Amsterdam. Huge cruise liners come from the North Sea to their terminal through the IJ, cargo ships coming from the Rhine canal head for the port of Amsterdam, and little passenger ferries cross to and fro non-stop to Amsterdam-Noord. It is hard to say exactly what the IJ is. A river? Part of the sea? A lake? None of these descriptions are really accurate. Before 1932, when the front-line dyke in the north of Holland had not yet been built, the IJsselmeer east of Amsterdam was still the Zuiderzee, part of the North Sea. Het IJ was then an arm of the Zuiderzee, akin to a bay. It originally terminated in the dunes west of Amsterdam; direct access to the open North Sea was first achieved in 1876 with the North Sea Canal. At the same time a dam and the Oranje sluices were built in the north of Amsterdam to separate the IJ from the IJsselmeer. Today the IJ is usually described as a river. Its water is slightly

Masters of the royal wave: Willem Alexander and Máxima with their daughters on Koningsdag

salty, but it is not officially regarded as seawater. Herring and other sea fish nevertheless feel absolutely at home in it.

# HEAVE-HO

You can see these beams on almost every house, whether 4 or 400 years old: beams for a hoist. Usually the beams with their attached hooks stick out from the house fronts above a window in the roof. They are by no means historic artefacts as they are still used today. The stairs in Amsterdam's houses are extremely steep and narrow, which makes it almost impossible to take large items to the upper floors. Instead residents hire a pulley from a removal company, attach it to the beam, hoist up wardrobes, pianos and anything else that is bulky, and haul them into the flat through a window.

# HOME ON THE WATER

Sometimes they look well kept, sometimes shabby; some are old barges that have been converted, others look like floating bungalows. 2,400 houseboats bob up and down on the city canals, especially Singel and Prinsengracht. In the 1950s, it was students who first hit on the idea that disused boats would make excellent places to live. Nowadays, they are home to eccentrics and people who have fallen in love with the idea of living on the water. The city authorities, however, have always been reluctant to accept these floating domiciles, and it is now practically impossible to get a mooring permit for a new houseboat.

# ROYALS

The Netherlands is a constitutional monarchy. But, this has not always been the case. Although the house of Orange-Nassau has ruled since 1572, Holland

The Dutch are not short on ideas: an automated snack bar with a drive-in for boats

was initially a republic after the wars of liberation against Spain. For some 200 years, the Orange rulers were only governors. The first king, Willem I, did not ascend the throne until 1815, following the withdraw of Napoleon's forces.

It may seem surprising that the pragmatic Dutch still allow themselves the luxury of a royal family. But just like her mother Juliana, who died in 2004 and was known to be particularly close to her people, Queen Beatrix (b. 1938), who succeeded to the throne in 1980 and abdicated in 2013, is very popular. Her former role as the darling of the Dutch people has now been taken over by her daughter-in-law, Máxima (b. 1971), who steals the show when she makes public appearances with her husband, King Willem-Alexander (b. 1967). Blonder than many Dutch women and always clad in stylish designer clothes, this Argentinean commoner is always smiling. Whenever the royal couple and their three daughters Amalia (b. 2003), Alexia (b. 2005) and Ariane (b. 2007) make an appearance on TV, the viewing figures spike.

# HOT & CRISPY

*Kroket, frikandel, loempia* and *patat oorlog* – these are the stars of Amsterdam's snacking scene. All of them are deep-fried and deliciously unhealthy. Some, like *loempia* (a cigar-shaped spring roll with hot and sweet chilli sauce), *bamischijf* (spicy noodles, deepfried and pressed into disk shape) and *patat oorlog* (French fries with mayonnaise, peanut sauce and onions) reveal gastronomic influences from the Dutch colonial past. But *nieuwe haring* (lightly salted herring, also known as *matjes*), which is as Dutch as Dutch can be, is also part of a flourishing fast-food culture. These herring are seldom eaten as a main course but usually as a snack in between meals bought from a street stall.

The zenith of Amsterdam's culture of snacking is the so-called *automatiek*, a machine for selling hot and greasy foods. Behind little doors, cheese soufflés, meatballs and croquettes are waiting for someone to throw a few euros into the slot, open the door and devour them. The best-known chain of snack bars with *automatiek* is called *Febo*. It was founded way back in 1941 and is represented on almost every corner in Amsterdam. Connoisseurs swear by the home-made INSIDER TIP *shrimp and meat croquettes of the Holtkamp bakery* at number 15 Vijzelgracht, which can also be found among the starters on the menus of some good Amsterdam restaurants.

# X XX

In many places in Amsterdam you see a symbol consisting of three crosses, one above the other. It adorns not only the crown on the top of the Westertoren, but also the gables of canal-side houses and especially the little brown posts known as Amsterdammertjes that separate the pavement from the road in the city centre. Some visitors speculate that they have something to do with the red light district and X-rated films – and in many shops you can buy humorous souvenirs that play on this association. In reality, however, they are the three St Andrew's crosses, which have been part of the city coat of arms since the Middle Ages. It is not clear why the coat of arms features these crosses. It may be connected to the fact that most Amsterdammers were once fishermen like St Andrew. Beginning in 1505, all ships registered in Amsterdam were required to fly the flag with the three crosses.

# CURTAIN UP!

Very tall windows without curtains are not an unusual sight on Amsterdam's canals. Many visitors express surprise at the openness of the Dutch, while others tell of a historic tax on curtains that prompted the thrifty Amsterdammers to do without. This tax is pure myth. It is true that there was a window tax in the 19th century, but this was only related to the number of windows, not how they were decorated. It is more probable that the way the houses on canals were constructed made curtains unnecessary. On the street side of the raised ground floor, there was usually a reception room designed to impress guests and those passing by were welcome to take a peek. The private living rooms lay behind it, shielded from prying eyes. Others attribute the lack of curtains to the Calvinist religion because a good Calvinist had nothing to hide and therefore let everyone look inside his home. In view of the high-class designer furniture that can often be seen behind the windows of expensive houses on the canals, the owners' pride in their possessions might also offer an explanation. However, these displays really only attract the attention of foreign visitors, as one of the Calvinist rules of the game is never to stare through other peoples' windows, however open to public gaze they may be.

# SIGHTSEEING

**CITY WHERE TO START?**

Dam (128 B3) (*ⅢⅡ F3*) is the ideal starting point for exploring Amsterdam. This historic main city square on the axis running from the main station is the site of the Natio-naal Monument, the Royal Palace and the Nieuwe Kerk, but also the long-established department store Bijenkorf. It also marks the start of the Kalverstraat shopping street. You can park a car at the Bijenkorf store, but it is cheaper and less stressful to walk five minutes from the station or take a tram; lines 1, 2, 4, 5, 9, 13, 14, 16, 17 and 24 stop at the Dam.

Amsterdam has no fewer than 8500 protected buildings. Most of them are situated within comfortable walking distance of the city centre – either in de Wallen, the oldest district of the city, or along the canal rings.

Nobody should leave Amsterdam without taking a proper walk along Singel, Herengracht, Keizersgracht or Prinsengracht. Some of the newer or less well-known quarters of the city are also worth a detour. If you want to get a good overall impression of Amsterdam to start with, go up the ⚲ tower of the Westerkerk.

If you have come to explore the rich his-tory of Dutch art, then the decision is easy: the Rijksmuseum, Van Gogh Mu-seum and Stedelijk Museum, the three

Art is everywhere – in venerable museums, hyper-modern exhibition venues and quirky little galleries

most important in the country, are all situated on one square called (what else?) Museumplein. All three museums have undergone extensive renovations in recent years. The futuristic, bathtub-shaped annex to the Stedelijk Museum was made the greatest splash – like everyone else, you'll either love it or hate it. Irrespective of what you make of this architecture, the collections in these three museums are definitely first rate.

Amsterdam's museums are not only for art lovers. If handbags, history or sim-

ply strange and unusual collections are your thing, there is a museum here for you. And if you do not feel like walking everywhere, the *Canal Bus* will take you from door to door. Its three routes include stops at all the important museums. For 24 euros, you can hop on and off wherever you want for twenty four hours and benefit from discounted admission prices at a number of museums.

If you plan to visit several museums, it's worth buying a *Museumkaart (MK, www.museumkaart.nl)*. This annual

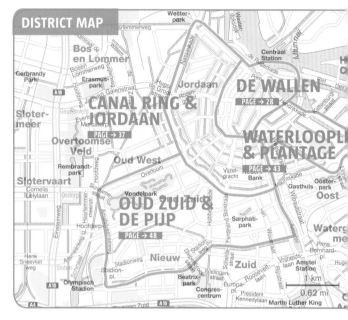

**DISTRICT MAP**

The map shows the location of the most interesting districts. There is a detailed map of each district on which each of the sights described is numbered.

pass gets you into most of the major museums of the Netherlands at no additional charge. For adults the standard price is around 55 euros, but those under 18 pay only 29.95 euros. The pass is sold at every museum and can be used straight away. Museums that accept the *Museumkaart* are marked in this travel guide with the letters MK in brackets next to the admission price.

The *I amsterdam City Card* is also worth considering because it offers admission to the best-known museums in Amsterdam and free public transport for one, two or three days (see p. 118).

# DE WALLEN

**Amsterdam's medieval centre *De Wallen* takes its name from the four oldest canals in the city: the former defensive moats called Voorburgwal and Achterburgwal, which surrounded the "oude" and "nieuwe zijde" (the old and the new side) of the city.**

Around these canals – only two still exist because those on the "new side" were filled in – one of the most colourful and controversial neighbourhoods have grown up, including the red light district and Chinatown. Here you will find the oldest church and the best Asian snack stalls, but also Amsterdam's dirtiest corners. This makes for a very diverse street scene: tourists, junkies, authentic Amsterdammers, shoppers, Chinese residents, prostitutes and students go about their business between neon signs and canal-side houses, which seem much less smart here than on the upmarket Canal Ring. The houses were built between the 14th and 16th centuries, when there were no strict building regulations. As a result some have a wide façade, others a narrow one, some are tall and others low, some are imposing and others extremely crooked. It pays to stop for a while and look up at the façades above the shops or to take refuge from the hurrying crowds on Kalverstraat in the peace of the Begijnhof. Don't be shy about walking through narrow passages or taking a look in a little courtyard because this is how you can discover hidden gems such as the restaurant Blauw aan de Wal or the book market behind the Oudemanhuispoort. The hubs of this richly varied hustle and bustle are the squares Dam, Spui, Rembrandtplein and Nieuwmarkt.

### ■ AMSTERDAM DUNGEON
(128 B4) (Ⓜ F4)

For those who like it macabre: an exhibition to send a shiver down your spine about the dark side of Amsterdam's history, including live demonstrations and a ghost train. *Daily 11am–5pm | admission 22 euros | Rokin 78 | www.the-dungeons. nl | tram 4, 9, 16, 24 Rokin*

### ② AMSTERDAM MUSEUM
(128 A–B4) (Ⓜ F4)

Amidst the throngs of shoppers on Kalverstraat, a Baroque gate marks the entrance to the city museum. Head right in and discover the surprisingly large courtyard of this 17th-century

**MARCO POLO HIGHLIGHTS**

building that was once an orphanage. A very entertaining and interactive exhibit on the history of the city awaits inside. After an hour at the museum, you'll come to understand how entrepreneurialism, freedom of thought, civic consciousness and creativity have shaped the city for centuries. *Daily 10am–5pm | admission 12.50 euros (MK) | Kalverstraat 92 | www.amsterdammuseum.nl | tram 1, 2, 4, 5, 9, 14, 16, 24 Spui or Rokin*

### ▣ BEGIJNHOF ★ ●
(128 A4) (*ฌ F4*)

An oasis of peace and quiet in the buzzing city centre – at least if you come on a weekday and a busload of tourists hasn't just arrived. White-painted houses with lovingly tended, tiny front gardens are grouped around a small church and a few chestnut trees. When it was founded in 1346, the Begijnhof, was located on the edge of

town. It was a place of residence fo single women who wished to live in religious community but not becom nuns. They mainly devoted themselve to caring for the aged. Two fires almos completely destroyed the Begijnhof i the 15th century. The buildings as the are today largely date from the 17t century. The house at number 34, b contrast, was built around 1470 and thought to be the oldest wooden hous in the Netherlands. Opposite the En lish Presbyterian chapel, a 17th-centur Catholic INSIDER TIP *secret church* hidden within two residential building About 100 people still live in the Begij hof – but the last beguine died in 197 *Daily 9am–5pm | entrances on Spui an Kalverstraat | tram 1, 2, 5 Spui*

### ▣ BEURS VAN BERLAGE
(128 C2) (*ฌ G3*)

This brick building presides like a castl over Damrak, and its tall tower can b

Still-life with a beguine: the Begijnhof is as peaceful as a village during the week

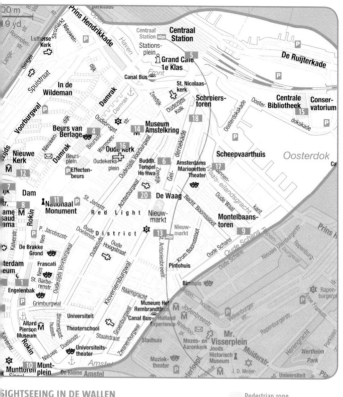

seen from afar. The commodity and stock exchange, built between 1897 and 1903 to plans made by the architect Hendrik Petrus Berlage, is regarded as a cornerstone of modern architecture in the Netherlands thanks to its plain façade and openly visible structural elements.

At first, the building's owners were not at all pleased with the exchange. They would have preferred a prestigious-looking building in the neo-Renaissance style like the Rijksmuseum or the main station. However, a historical architectural style was exactly what master builder Berlage wanted to move away from. He invited some of his artist friends to decorate the building with contemporary ornamentation and works of art. Murals, sculptures, decorative ironwork and mottos complement the massive architecture and make the exchange building as a whole a work of art. The building can only be toured during exhibitions and events. On the other side of the street, be sure to take a look at the well-lit INSIDERTIP *Beurspassage*, which was turned into a collective masterpiece by a number of artists in 2016. Although most of the decorative features seem to be historic at first glance, a closer look reveals chandeliers made of old bikes and sconces that look like paper cones for French fries. | *www.beursvanberlage.nl* | *tram 4, 9, 16, 24 Dam*

### 5 CENTRAAL STATION
(129 D1) (*[] G3*)

The main station was built in 1889 in neo-Renaissance style by Petrus J. H. Cuypers, the architect of the Rijksmuseum. This "Travellers' Palace" is supported by more than 10,000 tree trunks that were rammed into the sandy ground. Hungry travellers and visitors should check out the new INSIDERTIP Concourse on the north side of the station. It is lined with restaurants that offer something for every taste, ranging from huge burgers and Vietnamese soups to Mexican burritos.

Make sure to check out the bike tunnel on the western end of the station that is decorated with a tiled mural depicting sailboats designed by Irma Boom. This artwork caused quite an stir when the tunnel first opened because a ship from the rival city of Rotterdam is depicted front and centre. Free ferries depart for Amsterdam-Noord from the rear side of the station. *The main station is the central terminus for trams, buses, boat tours and museum boats.*

### 6 CENTRALE OBA ●
(132 A5) (*[] H3*)

Amsterdam's public library is a real magnet for visitors. This impressive new building on Oosterdok island is entirely furnished with the work of Dutch designers. On the upper floor there is a good self-service restaurant with a ☀ terrace that offers a wonderful view of the historic city centre. *Daily 10am–10pm | Oosterdokskade 143 | 5 min. walk from the main station*

# TIME TO CHILL

Massages, beauty treatments and saunas make for relaxation at its finest. When the ambience is just right, there is almost nothing better for body and soul — for example in the ● *Sauna Déco* **(128 A2)** *([] F3) (Mon, Wed–Sat noon–11pm, Tue 3–11pm, Sun 1–7pm | Herengracht 115 | tel. 020 6 23 82 15 | www.saunadeco.nl | tram 13, 17 Nieuwezijds Kolk)* at the heart of the Canal Ring. The interior was brought here from a 1920s Paris department store that was demolished. You can treat yourself to a relaxing hydro massage, a steam bath, a manicure or a foot massage in style and take a break from the pampering in the comfortable lounge with a snack.

A royal palace with a common past: the Great Hall in the palace that was once the town hall

## CHINATOWN (129 D2–3) (*Ⓜ G3*)

Amsterdam's Chinatown is the district around Zeedijk and Nieuwmarkt. In the early 20th century many Chinese sailors came to the city. Some stayed and brought their families to join them. The Chinese still form a close-knit community and keep up their traditions. In Chinatown you will find authentic Chinese restaurants as well as Chinese bakeries, fashion boutiques and medical practices. The colourful icing on the cake is the Buddhist *Fo Guang Shan He Hua Temple (Tue–Sat noon–5pm, Sun 10am–5pm | Zeedijk 106–118 | metro Nieuwmarkt)*, which is open to the public at no charge.

## KONINKLIJK PALEIS ● (128 B3) (*Ⓜ F3*)

At first sight, the plain grey building on the Dam with its curtained windows does not look like a royal palace. Sometimes, it is a tad disrespectfully referred to as Holland's biggest broom closet". Origi- nally, it was not built as a palace, but rather as a town hall. Jacob van Campen was the architect of this building in the classical style, erected between 1648 and 1655. 13,659 piles had to be driven into the ground to support the weight of the imposing structure of Bentheim stone. A huge frieze depicting all kinds of sea monsters adorns the main façade. On the inside, the huge and elaborately decorated Great Hall is the main attraction. But a chill will probably run down your spine in the smaller but no less impressive Vierschaar, a historic Dutch tribunal where death sentences were once passed down. The city of Amsterdam did not turn over its town hall to the monarchy until 1930. The main residence of the House of Orange is in The Hague – the king only stays in the Amsterdam palace for receptions, and it is not open to the public when he is in residence. For up-to-date opening times, see *www.paleisamsterdam.nl or tel. 020 6 20 40 60 |*

*admission 10 euros (MK) | tram 1, 2, 4, 5, 9, 13, 14, 16, 17, 24 Dam*

### ⬛9 MADAME TUSSAUD'S
**(128 B3) (*ₘ F3*)**

If you always wanted to stand next to Rembrandt, Kylie Minogue or King Willem-Alexander and are prepared to pay a lot of money for the pleasure, you can make your dreams come true among the wax figures of celebrities from all walks of life, some of them more real-looking than others in this museum. *Daily 10am–7pm | admission 24.50 euros | Dam 20 | tram 4, 9, 14, 16, 24 Dam*

### ⬛10 MONTELBAANSTOREN
**(129 E3–4) (*ₘ H4*)**

This little tower is one of the most popular photo motifs in town. It was built in the 16th century as part of the defences on the Oude Schans canal which formed the outer boundary of the city at the time. As legend has it the bells once began to peel at odd times, earning the tower its nickname "Malle Jaap" ("crazy Jacob"). Since 1878 Amsterdam's waterworks have used it to monitor the water level and the circulation in the canals. *Oudeschans 2 | metro Nieuwmarkt*

### ⬛11 MUNTTOREN (128 B5) (*ₘ G4*)

In the hustle and bustle at the junction of Kalverstraat, Singel and Reguliersbreestraat, it is easy to overlook the Mint Tower, which dates to 1620, despite the fact that it once played a very important role in the city's defences. When the city of Dordrecht, which had the right to mint coins, was in danger of being occupied by French forces in 1672, gold and silver

A rather lovely place to monitor the canals: Montelbaanstoren with its lovely view of the water

coins were minted here for just a few months. *Muntplein 1 | tram 4, 9, 14, 16, 24 Muntplein*

## 12 NATIONAAL MONUMENT (128 B3) (*⏃ F3*)

The national monument is located on the Dam, opposite the palace. This 22-metre high (72 ft.) obelisk, inaugurated in 1956, commemorates the victims of German occupation and is a monument to liberation and peace. In 1995 there was a bit of a scandal when it was found to be in need of restoration, and the only firm able to carry out the work turned out to be German. *Tram 4, 9, 14, 16, 24 Dam*

## 13 NIEUWE KERK ★ (128 B3) (*⏃ F3*)

The impressive Nieuwe Kerk on the Dam is Amsterdam's most famous church. It is not as new as its name suggests. Construction in the late Gothic style began in the 15th century, when the city had outgrown its first line of fortifications and the Oude Kerk had become too small. The church gained its present form around 1540 after several fires and renovations. Only 38 years later, during a campaign of iconoclasm known as the *Beeldenstorm*, Protestants removed every last statue and altar, meaning that the interior makes an extremely sober impression today. The main attraction in the church is the pulpit, adorned with elaborate carvings that took the sculptor Albert Jansz Vinckenbrinck 15 years to complete.

The Nieuwe Kerk has no tower. Although foundations were laid for one in 1565, political turbulence and iconoclastic fervour prevented construction. By the time things had quietened down, the city council no longer wanted a tower that would have been higher than the dome of the new town hall (today's palace), which certainly speaks to the historic balance of power in Amsterdam. As a compromise, the site of the town hall was pushed back to allow space for at least the high transept of the church to border the square.

Today, the church is used as an exhibition space, which has hosted a variety of exhibits with subjects ranging from Muslim art to Marilyn Monroe. The Nieuwe Kerk is still used for the coronations of Dutch Kings and Queens, such as the ceremony for King Willem-Alexander in 2013. *Daily 10am–5pm | admission varies by exhibit | Dam | www.nieuwekerk.nl | tram 1, 2, 4, 5, 9, 13, 14, 16, 17, 24 Dam*

## 14 NIEUWMARKT ★ (129 D3) (*⏃ G4*)

Many street cafés and pubs line the Nieuwmarkt, which surrounds the old weighing house between the red light district and Chinatown. The chairs and tables are all set up so that guests can people-watch to their heart's content. During the day, the market stalls are full of life, but at night, the crowds throng toward the red light district. On a sunny summer day, Nieuwmarkt is the perfect place to catch a few last rays with a glass of wine just before sunset. *Metro Nieuwmarkt*

## 15 ONS' LIEVE HEER OP ZOLDER (128 C2) (*⏃ G3*)

Nothing on the outside of this old canal house in the red light district seems to tell what is hidden inside. On the lower floors it appears to be a perfectly normal 17th century merchant's house. Climb up and down the stairs to explore the nooks and crannies of this canal house and get a taste for what life was like in the Golden Age for the city's burghers.

The main attraction, however, is hidden away under the roof: a three-storey Catholic INSIDER TIP *secret church*, built in 1661 and fitted out with a high altar and two galleries. As the ruling Calvinists had prohibited Catholics from practising their religion openly, worshippers had to sneak into the house by a side entrance. *Mon–Sat 10am–5pm, Sun 1–5pm | admission 10 euros (MK) | Oudezijds Voorburgwal 38 | www.opsolder.nl | 10 min. walk from the main station*

### 16 OUDE KERK ★ (128 C3) (*ΩＪ G3*)

Built around 1300, Amsterdam's oldest church is located in the red light district. The neighbouring houses crowd around the church, and the eclectic mix of goings-on that take place inside them could not be more typical of the canal city: while hipsters sip their soy lattes in a café next to red-lit windows showcasing scantily dressed women, children attend nursery just a few doors down The church itself is a patchwork of different architectural styles because it underwent renovations and modifications from 1350 onward. Several chapels were added in the 15th century, followed by the raising of the nave ceiling and a taller tower in the 16th century. Nowadays, concerts and travelling modern art exhibitions are hosted in the church. *Mon–Sat 10am–6pm, Sun 1pm–5pm | admission 7.50 euros (MK) | Oudekerksplein 23 | www.oudekerk.nl | tram 4, 9, 16, 24 Damrak*

### 17 SCHEEPVAARTHUIS (129 D–E3) (*ΩＪ H3*)

At first sight, the "house of seafaring" almost looks like the setting for a Batman film. Forbidding, and even a bit threatening, it stands on Binnenkade to the east of the main station. It was built in 1916 and is an early example of the brick Expressionism of the 1920s which was to become the famous style of the "Amsterdam School". Stylised maritime figures and other ornamental elements decorate its façade. Originally the seat of the most important shipping companies, it has housed the *Grand Hotel Amrâth* since 2007 *(see p. 86)*. *Prins Hendrikkade 108–114 | 5 min. walk from the main station*

### 18 SCHREIERSTOREN (129 D2) (*ΩＪ G3*)

From the battlements of this semi-circular defensive tower built in 1484, sailors' wives supposedly wept as ships departed. Although a 17th-century gable stone tells this story, it is not true. The tower was originally called *schreyhoekstoren* because it sits where two canals meet at a sharp angle *(schreye hoek)*. Henry Hudson sailed from this tower – the subject of many paintings – to North America in 1609, where he discovered Manhattan and founded New Amsterdam, later known as New York. The Hudson River and Hudson Bay are named after him. The tower houses a INSIDER TIP cosy café. *Prins Hendrikkade 94/95 | 5 min. walk from the main station*

### 19 SPUI (128 A5) (*ΩＪ F4*)

Lined by old Amsterdam pubs such as *Café Luxembourg, Zwart* and INSIDER TIP *Café Hoppe*, whose dark wood-panelled interior with sand on the floor first opened in 1670, Spui is regarded as the city's most traditional square. On Fridays, it is home to a *book market*. *Tram 1, 2, 5 Spui*

### 20 DE WAAG (129 D3) (*ΩＪ G4*)

Amsterdam's oldest secular building stands in the middle of Nieuwmarkt. It is the former weighing house, now home to an institute for new media and a café restaurant. Built in 1488 as a city gate, it was converted into a weighing house when the Canal Ring was constructed in the 17th century. All Dutch cities had such calibrated public scales where merchants could weigh cheese wheels and other goods to make sure that there was no swindling going on.

Beneath the roof of this building, the guild of surgeons installed a so-called *Anatomical Theatre*, which has been preserved. It can only be viewed during events held by the media institute. At one of the many public dissections that took place in the Anatomical Theatre, Rembrandt painted his famous "Anatomy Lesson of Dr Tulp" (1632), which now hangs in The Hague in the Het Maurits-huis museum. *Metro Nieuwmarkt*

# CANAL RING & JORDAAN

**The completely preserved historic ★ *Canal Ring* is Amsterdam's biggest attraction – quite literally.**

The old canals, Singel, Herengracht, Keizersgracht and Prinsengracht, as well as countless smaller canals at right angles to these, form a semi-circle around the medieval city centre. In an area of some three square miles there are 160 canals and 600 bridges. After decades of trying, the city was finally able to get the canal ring listed as a Unesco World Heritage Site in 2010.

Around the year 1600 Amsterdam had become extremely wealthy through

Van der Mey Hall in the Scheepvaarthuis seems to resemble Batman's Gotham City

overseas trade. The beginning of the Golden Age was accompanied by a population boom. Within a mere 50 years, the number of residents increased fourfold. The old core of the city became too crowded and construction began on the Canal Ring, one of the most spectacular urban building projects at the time. Its innovative features were not only the spacious layout of the canals, but also the fact that trees were planted on the banks. Criminals, vagrants and day labourers were brought in to do the digging. Rich merchants built their new residences and warehouses on these waterways, which had originally been made to drain the land. Building plots on the canals, however, were expensive. As the purchase price and later taxation were based on the width of the plot, most houses were built with a narrow front, but then extended to the back. Herengracht, the "canal of gentlemen" was named after the well-to-do merchants. Keizersgracht honours Emperor ("Kaiser") Maximilian I, whose crown Amsterdam was permitted to include in its coat of arms, and Prinsengracht got its name from the princes of the House of Orange. By 1680, the plan to enlarge the city had been completed, and the Canal Ring was encircled by a defensive moat on the site of what is today Stadhouderskade.

The Canal Ring with its grand old burghers' houses is still one of the best addresses in Amsterdam, even if many of these former dwellings are now home to legal practices and private banks. The high curtainless windows offer a glimpse into the luxurious interiors of these old houses.

*Jordaan*, once a district for the poor, was built at about the same time as the Canal Ring. It is less upmarket but no less picturesque, and it has a village-like feel. Working-class families once had to live in damp basements in this quarter now populated by many intellectuals and artists ● as well as galleries and design studios. It was not until after the Second World War that conditions in Jordaan improved and the legendary neighbourhood spirit arose that inspired the sentimental songs still played in some of the "brown cafés" in Amsterdam's most *gezellig* (friendly and sociable) district.

The best way to visit the historic Canal Ring: by boat

### ◼ AMSTELKERK

**(136 B1) (⌘ G5)**

True to the idea that sometimes nothing is as permanent as a temporary solution, the wooden Amstelkerk was built In 1669, when there was a shortage of churches on the new Canal Ring. It was

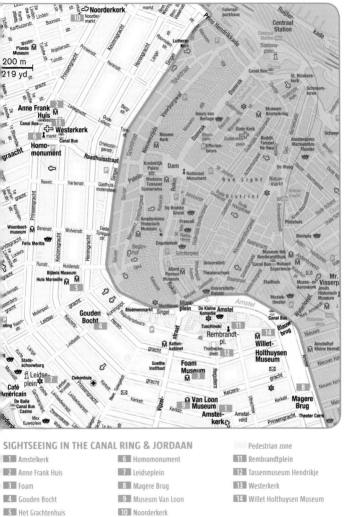

## SIGHTSEEING IN THE CANAL RING & JORDAAN

1. Amstelkerk
2. Anne Frank Huis
3. Foam
4. Gouden Bocht
5. Het Grachtenhuis
6. Homomonument
7. Leidseplein
8. Magere Brug
9. Museum Van Loon
10. Noorderkerk
11. Rembrandtplein
12. Tassenmuseum Hendrikje
13. Westerkerk
14. Willet Holthuysen Museum

Pedestrian zone

supposed to be replaced by a stone structure at a later time, but this never happened. Instead, this plain white church without a tower that looks a bit like a cowshed still stands on Amstelveld. The open space in front of the church with its old trees, playground and outdoor cáfe seating is one of the cosiest spots in Amsterdam. It is also home to a INSIDER TIP flower market with non-tourist prices on Monday mornings. *Amstelveld 10 | tram 4 Prinsengracht*

## ▨ ANNE FRANK HUIS ★
(131 D4) (𝄞 F3)

"Dear Kitty...": readers the world over recognise the words at the start of the entries in Anne Frank's diary. The spirited Jewish girl lived in hiding for two years during the Second World War with her family in this back-yard house on Prinsengracht – only to be deported at the last minute to Bergen-Belsen where she died as a result of the deplorable conditions.

Today the house is the headquarters of the Anne Frank Foundation and home to its museum. A secret door leads to the house at the back and the little flat in which the family was forced to live. Because of the museum's immense popularity, you can only tour the house between 9am and 3:30pm if you have booked online in advance. *April–Oct 9am–10pm; Nov–March, Sun–Fri 9am– 7pm & Sat 9am–9pm; closed on Yom Kippur | admission 9 euros | Prinsengracht 263 | annefrank.org | tram 13, 14, 17 Westermarkt*

## ▩ FOAM (128 B6) (𝄞 G5)

Fans of contemporary photo art should not miss out on this photography museum housed in a 19th-century canal house. Its changing exhibitions cover many different aspects of photography. The café in the basement is a great place for a sandwich afterwards. *Sat–Wed 10am–6pm, Thu–Fri 10am–9pm | admission 10 euros (MK) | Keizersgracht 609 | www.foam.nl | tram 16, 24 Keizersgracht*

## ▣ GOUDEN BOCHT ●
(131 E6) (𝄞 F–G 4–5)

The "golden arc" of the Herengracht stretches between Leidsestraat and Vijzelstraat. As the name suggests, these

# THE STARSHIP HAS LANDED

The Ajax Amsterdam football club (recognisable by white shirts with a red stripe) plays its home games in the Amsterdam Arena in the southeast of the city. The gigantic stadium looks like a spaceship that has landed on the grass. It has a retractable roof and holds almost 50,000 spectators. They need all those seats because the Amsterdammers go crazy when Ajax play. Football heroes like Johan Cruyff, Frank Rijkaard and Patrick Kluivert helped bring Ajax to fame. One thing that is surprising at first glance is that many fans wear the Israeli flag and paint a Star of David on their faces. Legend has it that Ajax was founded by Jews and remained a Jewish club for a long time. But, this myth has little to do with fact because the real goal of the fans is to distinguish themselves from the supporters of Feyenoord Rotterdam who tend towards the right wing. Ajax and Feyenoord are arch-rivals and matches between the two clubs, known as "De Klassieker", are a really big deal.

You can get hold of tickets for Ajax home games online, in the fan shop at the stadium or at Ticket Box sales outlets (usually kiosks and newsagents). You can also take a guided tour of the stadium *(daily, every 45 minutes between 11am and 5pm | 14.50 euros). Amsterdam Arena (0) (𝄞 0) (Arena Blvd. 1 | metro 50, 54 Strandvliet/ArenA | www.amsterdamarena.nl | www.ajax.nl)*

Don't expect to be able to visit the Anne Frank House without booking in advance

houses are noticeably larger and grander than most of the other canal buildings. They were built comparably late in the 17th century, when many merchants had already risen to become wealthy bankers who could afford double parcels. By then, symmetric neoclassic houses with columned entry portals were the favoured style of the day. Decorated like real palaces inside, they feature elaborate marble panelling and stucco details. Has your curiosity been piqued? Unfortunately you'll have to keep your distance from Number 502, the mayor's residence, but you are more than welcome to pop into Number 672, which is home to the *Museum Van Loon (see p. 42)*. Tram 16, 24 Vijzelstraat

### 5 HET GRACHTENHUIS
(131 E6) (*∅ F4*)

Listen to the story of our canals" is the motto at Het Grachtenhuis. In this patrician house built by Philip Vingboons in 1663, you can experience the design and construction of the canal ring up close, complete with historic maps, miniature canal houses, and a model of the city. *Tue–Sun 10am–5pm | admission 12 euros | Herengracht 386 | www.hetgrachtenhuis. nl | tram 1, 2, 5 Koningsplein*

### 6 HOMOMONUMENT (131 D4) (*∅ F3*)

Three rust-red marble slabs on the square in front of the Westerkerk became the world's first homosexual monument in 1987. It was placed there in memory of all persons who suffered persecution due to their homosexuality, first and foremost those who were victims of the Nazi occupation. *Tram 13, 14, 17 Westermarkt*

### 7 LEIDSEPLEIN (131 D6) (*∅ E5*)

If you are looking for action, this is the place. Tram bells ring, tourists pack the pubs, neon signs flash and street artists perform on this square at the heart of

A slim silhouette, lavishly illuminated: Magere Brug

the city. Cinemas, theatres, cafés and restaurants circle Leidseplein, which bursts with life at night, especially at weekends. Head to the INSIDER TIP balcony of the Stadsschouwburg for the best view of it all. *Tram 1, 2, 5, 6, 7, 10 Leidseplein*

### 8 MAGERE BRUG ● (136 C1) (*M G5*)

The Magere Brug looks like it belongs in a Van Gogh painting. Amsterdam's most famous bridge is particularly lovely at night when its lights twinkle like stars. *Kerkstraat | tram 4 Prinsengracht | metro Waterlooplein*

### 9 MUSEUM VAN LOON
(136 B1) (*M G5*)

Have you ever wondered what life was like for the city's upper crust in the 17th or 18th century? The answer awaits in this magnificent canal house. Built in 1671 for a wealthy merchant, the house was owned for a time by Rembrandt's pupil Ferdinand Bol. It was bought by the Van Loon merchant family in 1884. The reception rooms, salons, dining rooms and bedrooms are open to visitors. The Baroque INSIDER TIP canal garden, which is visible from the small salon, is a relic of bygone days. *Daily 10am–5pm | admission 9 euros | Keizersgracht 672 | tram 16, 24 Vijzelstraat*

### 10 NOORDERKERK
(128 A1) (*M F2*)

Although it is hard to believe, the Noorderkerk stood in the middle of a new housing area when it was first built. Today, it sits on Noordermarkt, one of Amsterdam's leafiest and most olde-worlde squares. At the rear, houses nestle up close to the church; not a single street approaches it at a right angle. Completed in 1623, the church is typically Protestant in that the pulpit is the focal point of its layout. *Mon 10:30am–12:30pm, Sat 11am–1pm | Noordermarkt 44 | 10 min walk from the main station*

### 11 REMBRANDTPLEIN
(128 C6) (*M G4–5*)

In the 1920s, Rembrandtplein was the hub of the city's art scene. Nowadays this square attracts tourists and night-life buffs because there is always something going on around the Rembrandt statue and the life-size sculptures depicting *The Night Watch*. *Tram 4, 9, 14 Rembrandtplein*

## 2 INSIDER TIP TASSENMUSEUM HENDRIKJE
(128 C6) *(⌖ G5)*

Handbags galore are on display at the Tassenmuseum, which documents the history of this fashion accessory from the 15th century to the present. Alongside its 4,000-piece collection and a pretty café, the museum runs a shop that sells designer handbags, so hold tight on your own purse strings. *Daily 10am–5pm | admission 12.50 euros | Herengracht 573 | www.tassenmuseum.nl | tram 4, 9, 14 Rembrandtplein*

## 13 WESTERKERK
(131 D4) *(⌖ F3)*

When it was completed in 1631, the Westerkerk, designed by Hendrick de Keyser, was the world's largest Protestant church. It is a light-filled white hall church with restrained ornamentation in the Renaissance style. However, the ☆ Westertoren, the 280-foot tower affectionately known as "Oude Wester" among Amsterdammers, is more famous than the church itself. It is the symbol of Jordaan and the subject of many songs. Its imperial-crown dome houses a glockenspiel with 49 bells. As it is the city's tallest tower, the superb view from the top makes the climb worthwhile. *Mon–Sat 11am–3pm, glockenspiel Tue noon–1pm, tower ascent April–June Mon–Fri 10am–6pm, Sat 10am–8pm; July–Sept Mon–Fri 10am–8pm, Sat 10am–8pm; Oct Mon–Fri 11am–5pm, Sat 10am–6pm | admission 7.50 euros | Prinsengracht 281/Westermarkt | tram 13, 14, 17 Westermarkt*

## 14 WILLET HOLTHUYSEN MUSEUM
(128 C6) *(⌖ G5)*

This merchant's house from 1687 accommodates the art collection of Abraham Willet (1825–88). His wife's fortune

Museum van Loon: see how a rich patrician family lived

enabled him to gather together an eclectic collection of art, crafts and fine furniture, which almost turned the home into a museum during his own lifetime. In 1889, his wife bequeathed the house with its collection to the city. The rooms are jammed full of ornate wall hangings, furniture, paintings and sculptures. *Mon–Fri 10am–5pm, Sat–Sun 11am–5pm | admission 9 euros | Herengracht 605 | www.willetholthuysen.nl | metro Waterlooplein*

# WATERLOO-PLEIN & PLANTAGE

**Around Waterlooplein there is a district that doesn't really exist any more. It was once the Jewish quarter, and the major-**

# WATERLOOPLEIN & PLANTAGE

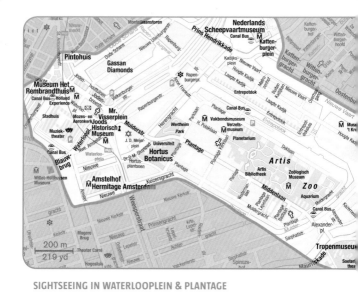

## SIGHTSEEING IN WATERLOOPLEIN & PLANTAGE

**ity of its inhabitants were deported and murdered during the Second World War. The only thing that remains today is the word "Mokum", the Yiddish word for home, which is still one of Amsterdam's nicknames.**

Beginning in the 17th century, many Jews resettled to the Netherlands because of the country's religious tolerance. Amsterdam's Jewish quarter was soon populated by both Ashkenazi (German descent) and Sephardic (Portuguese descent) Jews as well as a few unlucky, financially destitute Christians. During World War II, the Nazis brought an abrupt end to the city's flourishing Jewish community. Only 6,000 of Amsterdam's Jews survived the Holocaust. What remains today are several synagogues that are now home to the Jew-

ish Museum as well as some diamond cutting shops and kosher restaurant. The appearance of the quarter ha also changed over time. In the 1980 large-scale redevelopment efforts t revitalise this relatively downtrodden area left very little of the old building fabric intact.

Adjoining to the east is the more gen teel and leafy residential district D Plantage. When the Canal Ring wa laid out in the 17th century from west to east, it did not extend beyond the Amstel. Instead there were garden and shipyards to the east. It was no until the 19th century that they made way for a middle-class neighbourhood and a customs warehouse, the Entre potdok. Today, visitors come to thi green district mainly for the Tropenmu

...eum, the zoo or the botanical garden. However, it is also worth taking a look at the Entrepotdok with its old warehouses that have been converted into soft apartments.

## BLAUWBRUG (129 D6) (*ɷ G4*)

The sight of the Blauwbrug is a little bit reminiscent of the Pont Neuf in Paris. This elaborately decorated bridge across the Amstel was built in 1884. Its piers have the shape of the bows of ships, and the lanterns are topped by golden imperial crowns. *Amstelstraat/Waterlooplein | am 9, 14 | metro Waterlooplein*

## GASSAN DIAMONDS
(129 E4) (*ɷ H4*)

Amsterdam was once an international centre of the diamond-cutting trade. After World War II, this business declined in importance, but there are still a few workshops where diamonds are cut and polished. Many of those that offer tours are purely visitor attractions because the genuine workshops are not usually open to the public. Gassan Diamonds is the exception. In an imposing brick building dating from the late 19th century, 500 employees are engaged in polishing and selling these precious stones.

On the free tours, visitors follow the stone's path from a raw diamond to a polished gem, and it goes without saying that this is followed by a sales pitch. *Daily 9am–5pm | Nieuwe Uilenburgerstraat 173–175 | free admission | www.gassan.com | metro Waterlooplein*

## ⚫ HERMITAGE AMSTERDAM
(129 D6) (*ɷ G5*)

Since the famous Hermitage art museum in St Petersburg is bursting at the seams, some of its treasured artworks have been transferred to satellite museums in London, Las Vegas, and now Amsterdam. Changing exhibits featuring pieces from the main collection are

Since the Russian Hermitage has so many masterworks left, there's a branch in Amsterdam

on display in this former residence for the elderly dating to the 17th century. Don't forget to take a look at the old church hall, the regency room and especially the INSIDER TIP fully equipped historic kitchen, where meals were once prepared for the elderly residents. *Daily 9am–5pm | admission 17.50 euros | Nieuwe Herengracht 14 | www.hermitage.nl | metro Waterlooplein*

### 4 HORTUS BOTANICUS
*(129 E–F 5–6) (ΩΩ H4)*

As one of the oldest botanical gardens in the world, the Hortus is chock full of both plants and history. Over 300 years ago, Dutch doctors began planting this garden full of exotic herbs that merchants and mariners had brought back from their voyages to faraway places. This soon gave them a head start over their European colleagues in the field of tropical medicine. The old palm house is especially attractive, but don't miss out on the futuristic new greenhouse as well. In the *Hortus winkel*, you can buy flower bulbs and young shoots of rare plants. *Daily 10am–5pm | admission 8.50 euros | Plantage Middenlaan 2 | www.dehortus.nl | tram 9, 14, 20 Mr. Visserplein*

### 5 JOODS HISTORISCH MUSEUM
*(129 D5) (ΩΩ H4)*

No fewer than four synagogues from the 17th and 18th centuries are home to the Jewish Historical Museum, which lies at the heart of what was once the Jewish quarter. Glass-covered passages were added to connect them together as a part of a single museum. The permanent exhibit describes the culture and religion of the Jewish community in the Netherlands, including the history of the persecution of Jews. The temporary exhibits are usually a bit more light-hearted, with topics ranging from Jewish photography to Amy Winehouse. The JHM also has a children's museum.

## FIT IN THE CITY

You can do many things in Amsterdam – but probably not many people know that you can go windsurfing right in the city centre. Not on the canals, of course, but on the IJsselmeer. Book a private, 3-hour beginner's course for 125 euros or take part in a group course for 50 euros at *Surfcenter IJburg* **(0)** *(ΩΩ 0) (March–Sept Wed, Thu, Frt 2pm–sunset, Sat/Sun 11:30am–6:30pm | booking only via mailinfo@surfcenterijburg.nl | www.surfcenterijburg.nl | tram 26 IJburg, then 10 min. on foot)*. After that – if the wind is not too strong – you'll already glide over the waves all by yourself. If that's altogether too windy for you, you can swim in Amsterdam's most beautiful indoor pool right next to the Rijksmuseum. The ● *Zuiderbad* **(135 F2)** *(ΩΩ F6)* has not changed much since 1912. Even the original changing cubicles are still in use, and swimmers can continue to swim undisturbed in the Art Nouveau interior: two lanes are reserved for swimmers doing lengths on weekday mornings. *Mon 7am–6pm, Tue–Wed 7am–9am & noon–10pm, Th 7am–9am & noon–6pm & 8pm–10pm, Fri 7am–10pm, Sat 8am–3pm, Sun 10am–3:30pm | admission 3.40 euros Hobbemastraat 26 | tram 2, 5 Hobbemastraat; 7, 10 Spiegelgracht*

that is furnished like a Jewish family home.

You can try kosher specialities such as *Kugel* and *Latkes* in the museum café. *Daily 11am–5pm | admission 15 euros (MK) | Jonas Daniël Meijerplein 2–4 | www.jhm.nl | tram 9, 14 Mr. Visserplein | metro Waterlooplein*

### 6 PINTOHUIS (129 D4) (*Ø G4*)

This house was the subject of much dispute in the 1960s because, like many of the houses in the old Jewish quarter, it was supposed to be torn down. Originally built in 1605 by the Pinto family of Jewish bankers, protests saved it from the wrecking ball and it was then luckily turned into a public library. The beautiful 17th-century murals and ceiling paintings can still be admired in the entry hall. *Sint Antoniesbreestraat 69 | metro Nieuwmarkt*

### 7 REMBRANDTHUIS (129 D4–5) (*Ø G4*)

Rembrandt van Rijn (1606–69), the painter of *The Night Watch* was a talented artist, a troublemaker and a ladies' man all rolled into one, not to mention one of Amsterdam's most famous sons. Born in Leiden, the painter spent most of his life in the city of canals. His love life and his financial situation were subject to constant fluctuation. He bought this house in what was then the Jewish quarter in 1639. Money problems forced him to sell it in 1660 and move into a rented flat before dying a pauper in 1669.

His former house was converted into a museum in 1908. A modern annex houses the world's largest collection of etchings, copperplate engravings and drawings by Rembrandt. The old part of the house has been furnished as it might have looked in Rembrandt's time, including his studio. *Daily 10am–6pm | admission 13 euros (MK) |*

Glass ceilings in the Hortus Botanicus

*Jodenbreestraat 4–6 | www.rembrandthuis. nl | tram 9, 14 Mr. Visserplein | metro Waterlooplein*

### 8 SCHEEPVAARTMUSEUM (132 B5) (*Ø J4*)

The maritime museum, housed in what was once a naval arsenal dating from the 17th century, has a large collection of ships' models, old navigation instruments, weapons, charts and paintings that illustrate the glorious history of Dutch seafaring. It also features three interactive multimedia exhibits about whaling, the Golden Age and the port of Amsterdam today that are particularly geared towards children. The replica of the INSIDER TIP East Indies ship *Amsterdam* is also quite popular among

A replica, but every bit as impressive as the original: the East Indies ship *Amsterdam*

young guests. Visitors of all ages enjoy exploring what life was like as a sailor in the 18th century up close: The crew scurry round all day, busy unloading cargo, scrubbing the deck and singing sea shanties. The original *Amsterdam* didn't sail all the seven seas because it sank in a storm off the English coast on its maiden voyage. *Daily 9am–5pm | admission 15 euros (MK) | Kattenburgerplein 1 | www.scheepvaartmuseum.nl | bus 22, 48 Kadijksplein*

### 9 ■ TROPENMUSEUM ●
(137 E1) (*∅ J5*)

If you want to learn about the ointments that Mexicans use to massage away their headaches, what's popular on Philippine TV, or what kind of feathered masks were worn in Africa in the 19th century, then head to the Tropenmuseum. When it was founded in 1910, the museum displayed items brought back by the Dutch from their colonies in Southeast Asia and South America. Nowadays, such a colonial museum would no longer be considered politically correct, so the museum now provides a glimpse into the culture and everyday life in tropical and subtropical places. Take an entertaining trip around the world, stopping to appreciate cultural highlights of all kinds. *Tue–Sun 10am–5pm | admission 12.50 euros | Linnaeusstraat 2 | www.tropenmuseum.nl | tram 6, 9, 14 Mauritskade*

# OUD ZUID & DE PIJP

**To the southwest of Museumplein lies the upper middle-class district of Oud Zuid. Built in the 19th century, everything is this neighbourhood is a bit**

**more upscale than in the rest of the city.**

ondelpark, Amsterdam's "green lung", es on the northwestern edge of this district. Wealthy residents donated the funds or this park so that they could have a ree-filled view from the windows of their illas. Today Oud Zuid (the "Old South") emains one of Amsterdam's most exlusive districts. Property prices are only igher on the canal ring. It is home to exclusive designer shops, expensive resaurants and the city's best museums. To he east is INSIDER TIP *De Pijp*, which was uilt as a working-class quarter around he same time. Thanks to gentrification and urban renewal, the flats in the former enement buildings are now quite popuar among hipsters and young families. As ne of the most multicultural districts in he city, *De Pijp* offers a colourful array of rendy spots to eat, shop or head out on he town at night.

## ◼ HEINEKEN EXPERIENCE
(136 B2) (*ƉƉ F6*)

Although beer is no longer produced n the old Heineken brewery on Stadhouderskade, visitors can still discover the world of Heineken on an interactive tour. Two free *biertjes* cap off this brewery experience. *Mon–Thu 11am–5:30pm, Fri–Sun 10:30am–7pm | admission 18 euros | Stadhouderskade 78 | tram 16, 24 Heinekenplein*

## ◼ RIJKSMUSEUM ★ (135 F2) (*ƉƉ F5*)

Designed by the architect Pierre Cuypers, who also did the main station, the museum opened to the public in 1885. Thanks to its ornate style, it looks more like a castle or cathedral than a museum at first glance. This actually caused a bit of a stir when the building first opened because the Protestant king, Willem III, refused to step foot in "this palace fit for an arch-

bishop". But this doesn't seem to bother any of the 20 million visitors to the museum each year. The entrance is located in a bicycle and pedestrian tunnel under the building. Once you leave the modern foyer, the elaborately decorated walls of the historic exhibit halls serve as the backdrop for a veritable treasure trove of artworks featuring the Dutch Golden Age in particular. It almost seems as if the museum was built around Rembrandt's famous painting *The Night Watch*, which presides in all its glory at the end of the gallery

## LOW BUDGET

Every Wednesday at 12:30 pm in the *Concertgebouw* **(135 E3)** (*ƉƉ E6*) *(Concertgebouwplein 2–6 | www.concertgebouw.nl | tram 3, 5, 12, 16 Concertgebouw)* there is a free half-hour ● lunchtime concert. You still need a ticket, though, so be sure to get there early because the queues are long!

Climb up the stepped roof of the green *NEMO* **(129 F2)** (*ƉƉ H3*) *(Oosterdok 2 | 10 min. walk from the main station)* to get a fantastic panoramic view of the old quarter of Amsterdam without paying a penny. In summer you can sit comfortably on the beanbags in the café.

At the shop on Dam and other locations around the city, *Tours & Tickets*, **(128 B3)** (*ƉƉ G3*) *(Damrak 97 | www.tours-tickets.com | tram 4, 5, 9, 16 Dam)* sells tours as well as discount tickets for museums and other attractions. You can save 3.50 euros on admission to Madame Tussauds, for example.

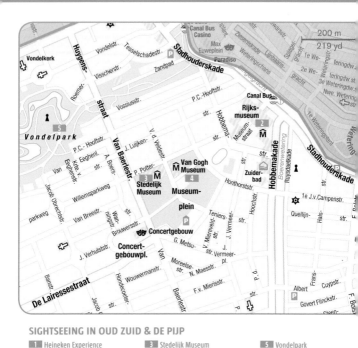

## SIGHTSEEING IN OUD ZUID & DE PIJP

1 Heineken Experience
2 Rijksmuseum
3 Stedelijk Museum
4 Van Gogh Museum
5 Vondelpark

of honour. The men who commissioned the painting in 1642 were not pleased with Rembrant's work because they felt that the members of Captain Frans Banning Cocq's shooting company had not been portrayed in a stately enough manner. But, this is actually what makes this piece such a masterpiece: it is incredibly dynamic and more realistic than the other militia paintings of the day. The other galleries exhibit the works of other Dutch painters such as Frans Hals, Jan Steen, Jacob van Ruisdael and Jan Vermeer. There is always a crowd in front of Vermeer's *Kitchen Maid* (1660) and *Woman in Blue Reading a Letter* (1662–64). Genre scenes such as these give a striking impression of life in middle-class Dutch households

of the 17th century – as does Jan Steen's *La Toilette* (1663), which depicts a young woman dressing in the morning. Do not miss out on the beautiful historic library that can be accessed from gallery 1.13. In the stairwell of the Philips wing, modern design meets history with the INSIDER TIP Shylight light sculpture by Studio Drift that creates a poetic ballet of light and shadows. *Daily 9am–5pm | admission 17.50 euros (MK), free for ages under 18 | Stadhouderskade 42 | www.rijksmuseum. nl | tram 2, 5 Rijksmuseum*

### 3 STEDELIJK MUSEUM

(135 E2) (ω E6)

The Stedelijk Museum holds one of the most significant collections of modern and contemporary art in the Netherlands. Among other things, it is famous for its galleries flooded with indirect natural light that create the perfect setting for works by Claude Monet, Mondrian, Karel Appel or Bruce Nauman. A bathtub-shaped futuristic annexe designed by the Amsterdam architects Benthem Crouwel was added to the 19th century main building in 2012. Its facade is wainscotted with seamless panels of a composite material that has only been used in aeroplane and ship building thus far. *Daily 10am–6pm, Fri until 10pm | admission 18 euros (MK) | Paulus Potterstraat 13 | www.stedelijk.nl | tram 2, 5 Van Baerlestraat & tram 3, 12 Museumplein*

### ◢ VAN GOGH MUSEUM ★
(135 E–F2) (*𝄞 E6*)

Just about everyone has seen images of the *Sunflowers*, *The Bedroom* or *The Potato Eaters*. Indeed, Van Gogh paintings are still some of the most expensive and most popular artworks of all time. The state-run Van Gogh Museum owns the world's largest collection of works by its namesake. This was made possible by the otherwise regrettable fact that almost none of Vincent van Gogh's (1853–1890) paintings found a buyer in his lifetime. He gifted them to his brother as a token of gratitude for the latter's financial support over the years. As a result, the paintings stayed in the family, which then bequeathed the 205 paintings and 500 drawings to the museum in 1963. The exhibition traces the eventful and tragic life of the artist from his early years in the Netherlands and his time in Paris and the south of France to his death in Auvers-sur-Oise.

In 1999, a new three-storey annexe was constructed next to the older part of the museum, originally built by Gerrit Rietveld. An underground passage connects the two buildings and houses the en-

A bright example of modern art: Installation by Dan Flavin at the Stedelijk museum

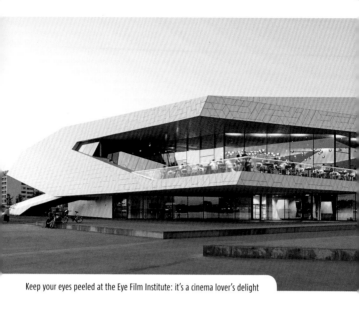

Keep your eyes peeled at the Eye Film Institute: it's a cinema lover's delight

trance to the museum. *Daily 9am–5pm, Fri until 10pm | admission 17 euros (MK) | Museumplein 6 | www.vangoghmuseum.nl | tram 2, 5 Van Baerlestraat & tram 3, 12 Museumplein*

### 5 VONDELPARK ★ ●
(134–135 C–E 2–3) (*∭ C–E 5–6*)

Don't come here looking for an oasis of peace and quiet. Vondelpark is less a green space than a meeting place, bicycle route, event venue and playground for Amsterdammers. Back in the 1960s, it was a magnet for hippies from all over the world who set up camp for a while until the police put an end to the squatting in 1975. But its origins were much more conventional. The 120-acre space, named after the Renaissance poet Joost van den Vondel, was the first public park in Amsterdam when it was created in 1877. Well-off citizens had got together to create an oasis of greenery

in front of their new villas to the south of the Canal Ring. Vondelpark is home to a *stage* where INSIDER TIP free open-air performances are held in summer. The *Blauwe Theehuis* sits directly behind it, where you'll find what is supposedly the only beer garden in Amsterdam. *Tram 1 Eerste Constantijn Huygensstraat & tram 3, 12 Van Baerlestraat*

# MORE SIGHTS

### A'DAM ★ (132 A2) (*∭ G2*)

The shell office tower on the north shore of the IJ stood empty for ages. Then, in 2015, the city sold it to a trio of investors from the dance scene, who have since turned it into a house that never sleeps. The club *Shelter* is located in the basement, while the burger restaurant *The Butcher Social Club* occupies the ground floor. The upper floors are

platform *(daily 10:30am–9pm | admission 12.50 euros, swing 5 euros extra)* on the roof that offers an incredible view of the city. For a real rush, let your legs dangle over the side of the building on Europe's highest swing. *Overhoeksplein 1 | www.adamtoren.nl | free ferry to Buiksloterweg from the north side of the main station*

### EYE FILM INSTITUTE (131 F2) (*𝄜 G2*)

It would be hard not to notice the futuristic white architecture of the *Eye Film Institute*, which stands on the north bank of the IJ just next to the A'DAM tower. It was designed by the Austrian architects at Delugan Meissl. Behind its sculptural façade lies the *Dutch film museum* with four cinema screens, 1,200 square metres (12,917 sq. ft.) of exhibition space, a museum shop and a waterfront café. In the *Filmlab* in the basement, you can comfortably watch a film from the collection in a yellow, two-seater ● mini cinema at no extra charge. The five-minute ⇖ crossing on the ferry is well worth it to watch a film or see an exhibition, or just to have a cup of coffee and watch what's happening on the water. *Daily 10am–9pm | IJpromenade 1 | www.*

home to the Hotel *Sir Adam* as well as office suites for music companies. In the round "throat" of the high-rise building, you'll find the award-winning *Moon* restaurant (with a revolving floor), topped by the cocktail bar *Madam*. But the biggest attraction is by far the ⇖ lookout

# IMMIGRANTS IN THE PARK

When you walk through Vondelpark in summer, you hear them squawking; in winter, when the branches of the trees are bare, you can see them clearly too: bright green parakeets. To be precise, they are ring-necked parakeets, a kind of Asian parrot that is commonly kept as a pet in Europe. In 1976 an owner released his pair in Vondelpark because they made too much noise. It didn't take the birds long to breed, and in Vondelpark there are several trees suitable for roosting at night. At sundown hundreds of parakeets gather there every day and stage a deafening, cacophonous concert. The local residents are none too keen on them, and neither are the Dutch animal protection authorities, as these immigrants compete with native birds for places to breed and supplies of food.

*eyefilm.nl | free ferry to Buiksloterweg
from the north side of the main station*

### IJBURG (139 D4) (*M 0*)

In the east of Amsterdam, a new archipelago is arising in the IJsselmeer. Seven artificial islands are being created to form the new district of IJburg, where it is planned that 45,000 people will one day live and work. Fans of modern architecture will find plenty to interest them here. Especially on the *Steigereiland,* the island nearest to the city, there are lots of curiosities, ranging from floating houses to yellow-tiled facades or a terraced house that looks like it was designed by Fred Flinstone. In summer the appealing improvised ● city beach of *Blijburg aan Zee* attracts many residents from the inner city to the eastern end of the new archipelago. *Daily 10am–10pm, closed Mon/Tue in bad weather | Pampuslaan 501 | www.blijburg.nl | tram 26 to the last stop (IJburg), then a 10 min. walk along Pampuslaan*

### INSIDER TIP ▶ NIEUWENDAM
(133 D–F 1–2) (*M–N1*)

If you want to get away from the noise and crowds of the city and see Dutch village life without taking a long journey, look no further than Nieuwendammerdijk. In what used to be a dyke village on the north side of the river IJ, one quaint little house stands next to another – all protected as historic buildings. In summer, it is pleasant to sit outside the small café by the harbour. *Bus 32 from Centraal Station Merelstraat*

### INSIDER TIP ▶ HET SCHIP 130 C1) (*M E1*)

This council housing block, shaped like a ship with its curves and other rounded features, was designed by Michel de Klerk in 1919 in keeping with the brick expressionist style. A little non-functional

tower graces one side, while the facade on the other has cigar-shaped bulges. It is also home to a *post office* and a *historic flat* with original furnishings as well as a *museum* that tells the story of the rather unique architectural style of the Amsterdam School. *Tue–Sun 11am–5pm | admission 12.50 euros (MK) | Oostzaanstraat 45 | bus 22, 48 Spaarndammerstraat*

# AROUND AMSTERDAM

### MARKEN (139 D3) (*M 0*)

With its green wooden houses, this village situated on an island in the IJsselmeer since the St Julian's Day flood of 1164 is like a picture-postcard of Holland. The little old houses snuggle together by the quayside, sailing boats bob up and down in the harbour, and some old ladies still wear traditional costume. In one of the harbour cafés you can drink coffee

Is the weather good and the city too full? Marken is just an hour from Amsterdam by train

with a view of the IJsselmeer or take a walk to the lighthouse. This place tends to attract tourists, especially at the weekend, but most of them tend to stick to the main streets in town. You can easily escape the crowds by making your way through the smaller side streets or taking a walk along the dyke to the lighthouse! The locals often head out for an evening pint at the little INSIDER TIP *Hof van Marken* hotel restaurant in the village centre *(Buurt II 5 | tel. 0299 60 13 00 | www.hofvanmark-en.nl). Bus 311 goes every half hour from the main station to Marken, journey time approx. 40 minutes. (return trip to Marken with the Waterlanddag-Kaart bought from the driver – 10 euros)*

If you feel like cycling there, you can get to Marken within two hours on a pleasant bike tour (approx. 22 km/14 miles). Behind the main station, take the ferry to IJplein, ride along Meeuwenlaan, turn right onto Nieuwendammerdijk, then stay on the dyke by the IJsselmeer. After the village of Uitdam turn right again

and pedal to Marken on the connecting dyke.

## ZANDVOORT AAN ZEE (138 A4) (*∅ 0*)

It takes barely half an hour by train to get to Zandvoort aan Zee, the North Sea resort on Amsterdam's doorstep. With its high-rises and faceless apartment blocks, this is not an attractive little place, but to make up for that there is a long, long sandy beach, and you only need to walk along it a short way to leave the town behind.

On warm summer weekends it can be crowded here, but outside the peak season you will have only the gulls for company. Typical features of Zandvoort are the fishing carts that tractors pull across the beach. They sell all sorts of deep-fried food and INSIDER TIP *delicious prawn rolls. Trains to Zandvoort every 30 min. from the main station, in winter change at Haarlem | return ticket 10.60 euros*

# FOOD & DRINK

**Cambodian, Ethiopian, Peruvian or Suri-namese – if you are willing to experiment, you can eat your way around the world in Amsterdam.**

And that's a good thing, some gourmets say, as Dutch food doesn't have a great reputation. The Calvinist tradition regarded all culinary pleasure as unnecessary, even sinful, and for centuries the people of Holland preferred to eat what was plain and nourishing. For example *stamppot:* mashed potato mixed with sausage or meat and cabbage. In recent years Dutch cooking has made progress. Chefs in good restaurants are inventing modern variations on local and seasonal specialities, rediscovering forgotten vegetables and experimenting with influences from all over the globe.

Dutch asparagus is excellent, and a bite of tender *hollandse nieuwe haring* can be relied on to convert those who were averse to matjes herring before. Specialities from the former Dutch colonies have also put down their roots in Dutch cuisine. Every child in Amsterdam knows what *nasi goreng* (rice with shrimps and chicken) and *saté* (skewered chicken with peanut sauce) are. The city's Indonesian restaurants are among the best in Europe. And in Chinatown you have opportunities to try authentic Chinese food that doesn't make compromises to please European palates.

There is a huge range of places to eat, with a snack bar or restaurant on almost every corner. Prices are relatively high and service is often not all it could be. But the

## Pancakes, Peking duck and bami goreng: Amsterdam's gastro scene is as multicultural as its people

waitstaff tends to be friendly and ready to tell a joke or two. If you are keeping the costs down, the cosy, typically Dutch *eetcafés,* where for the most part Dutch food with a Mediterranean touch is dished up, are a good bet. The more up-market *grand cafés* have either a modern or a old-world coffee-house atmosphere, and serve cakes and light meals all day. Normal *cafés* have the character of pubs. Asian snack bars, many of which can be found in Chinatown, will give you a cheap and tasty meal but are not places to linger.

The most popular drink is still a *biertje,* beer served in a small glass. Along with local brews like Amstel or Brandt, the sweeter Belgian beers are popular. In summer try *witbier*, a pale beer served with a slice of lemon. Don't forget to taste some *genever* – a spirit related to gin and made with juniper berries. The older it is, the spicier the taste.

At lunchtime, the options in Amsterdam are limited if you are looking for some-thing more than a sandwich or soup because the Dutch eat their main meal

Food courts offer a variety of yummy dishes from around the world

in the evening – traditionally as early as 6pm, now often later. Most restaurants don't open at midday, and many *eetcafés* close at 9:30pm.

## EETCAFÉS

### DE BAKKERSWINKEL ⊘
(130 C2) (*ⓜ E1*)

In a building that once belonged to the Westergasfabriek gasworks, a branch of the small Bakkerswinkel chain serves delicious salads and sandwiches made with regional organic ingredients when possible. *Closed Mon | Polonceaukade 1–2 | tel. 020 6 88 06 32 | tram 10 Van Hallstraat*

### MORLANG
(131 E6) (*ⓜ F4*)

Creative international cuisine and a young clientele in a wonderful canal-side house. The tables upstairs are more pleasant than in the basement. *Daily | Keizersgracht 451 | tel. 020 6 25 26 81 | tram 1, 2, 5 Keizersgracht*

### PIET DE LEEUW (136 B2) (*ⓜ F5*)

The very first *eetcafé* in Amsterdam. It is famous for steaks and enormous sole that are bigger than the plate. *Daily | Noorderstraat 11 | tel. 020 6 23 71 81 | tram 4, 9, 14 Rembrandtplein*

### INSIDER TIP WINKEL 43 (131 E3) (*ⓜ F2*)

The aroma of apples and cinnamon wafts through the air at Winkel 43, which is known for its *appeltaart mit slagroom*, a tart chock full of sliced apples. Especially on Saturdays, it is usually bursting at the seams. *Daily | Noordermarkt 43 | tel. 020 6 23 02 23 | tram 3 Marnixplein*

## FOOD COURT

### INSIDER TIP FOOD HALLS
(130 C6) (*ⓜ D4*)

Discover the whole world in just one hall. Twenty small snack stalls line up around the central bar in an old tram depot. From spring rolls and burgers to kofta, choose what you want and then meet up in the middle. *Sun–Thu 11am–*

*1:30pm, Fri/Sat 11am–1am | Bellamy-plein 51 | tram 7, 17 Kinkerstraat*

## GRAND CAFÉS

### CAFÉ AMÉRICAIN ★ (131 D6) *(ɰ E5)*

Elegant Art Nouveau café in the hotel of the same name. *Daily | Leidseplein 97 | tel. 020 5 56 30 10 | tram 1, 2, 5, 7, 10 Leidseplein*

### GRAND CAFÉ 1E KLAS
(129 D1) *(ɰ G3)*

Station cafés are not often inviting places, but this one is an exception, serving hamburgers and apple cake in historic fin-de-siècle surroundings. *Daily | Stationsplein 15 | platform 2b in the main station | tel. 020 6 25 01 31 | tram all routes to Centraal Station*

### DE JAREN (128 B5) *(ɰ G4)*

A large café with a restaurant upstairs serving good, plain food. In summer reserve a table on the ⛅ terrace, where you get a wonderful view of the city. *Daily | Nieuwe Doelenstraat 20–22 |*

*tel. 020 6 25 57 71 | tram 4, 9, 16, 24 Muntplein*

## RESTAURANTS: EXPENSIVE

### INSIDER TIP ▶ BLAUW AAN DE WAL
(128 C3) *(ɰ G3)*

In the middle of the red light district a narrow alley leads to this culinary oasis. The courtyard was once part of a monastery. Outstanding French cuisine and good service. *Closed Sun/Mon | Oudezijds Achterburgwal 99 | tel. 020 3 30 22 57 | metro Nieuwmarkt*

### C (137 D3) *(ɰ H6)*

C stands for Celsius at this restaurant in which the cooking temperatures in Michiel van der Eerde's renowned kitchen determine the menu. *Daily | Wibautstraat 125 | tel. 020 2 10 30 11 | www.c.amsterdam | metro Wibautstraat*

### ENVY (131 D5) *(ɰ E–F4)*

This hip restaurant with its stylish modern interior design in a long, nar-

---

# LOCAL SPECIALITIES

**appeltaart** – apple tart, cold or warm, served with slagroom (whipped cream)

**ba pao** – steamed Chinese rolls filled with meat or vegetables

**bitterballen** – deep-fried meatballs in breadcrumbs (photo left)

**erwtensoep** – thick pea soup with bits of sausage, accompanied by rye bread and bacon

**hollandse nieuwe** – young matjes herring

**kipsaté** – Indonesian skewered chicken with peanut sauce

**koffie verkeerd** – ("coffee the wrong way round") café au lait

**kroket** – deep-fried meat or shrimp croquettes

**loempia** – spring roll with or without meat

**mosselen** – mussels cooked in white wine, served with fries and mayonnaise

**nasi/bami goreng** – rice or noodles with shrimps and chicken (Indonesian speciality)

**oliebollen** – sweet dough with raisins fried in oil

**ontbijtkoek** – breakfast cake with honey, ginger, cinnamon and cloves

**ossenworst** – raw beef sausage, originally a Jewish speciality

**pannekoeken** – egg pancakes

**patat oorlog** – French fries with mayonnaise, peanut sauce and onions

**poffertjes** – mini-pancakes with icing sugar

**roti** – Indian or Surinamese flat bread filled with meat or vegetables

**stamppot** – mashed potato with sausage or meat and vegetables

**uitsmijter** – slices of bread with boiled ham, cheese and fried eggs (photo right)

**vla** – a thick vanilla pudding

row room sits on Prinsengracht. Guests sit together at a long counter to eat lots of delicious tidbits and drink a good vintage from the really extensive wine list. *Daily | Prinsengracht 381 | tel. 020 3 44 64 07 | tram 13, 14, 17 Westermarkt*

**GREETJE** ★ (129 E4) (*ØØ H4*)
Restaurant with a relaxed atmosphere hidden away in a side street. The style of cooking is truly unusual: modern Dutch cuisine, from baked black pudding to halibut with dune vegetables and crème

London City Airport
London City Airport
London E16 2PB
el: 020 7476 7707 Vat: 238 5548 36

| AMSTERDAM | MARCO | 7.99 |
|---|---|---|
| al | | £7.99 |
| a Contactless | | £7.99 |

Sale Transaction
VERIFIED BY DEVICE

ard No:      ************1683
ontactless
uth No:      545337
erchant ID: ***89243
ID:          A0000000031010
erminal ID: ****7132

Please retain for your records

1 item(s) sold
0 item(s) returned
ank you. Please retain your receipt
as proof of purchase.

04645261499388310821

08/2021 19:40:31 04645 0261 499388 FL

# WHSmith

EST·1792

0404526149938310821

brûlée with liquorice root. *Closed Mon | Peperstraat 23 | tel. 020 7 79 74 50 | metro Nieuwmarkt*

### GUTS & GLORY (128 C6) *(ЫФ G4)*

This small bistro near Rembrandtplein offers a different set menu (4 or 6 courses) each week that is full of surprises ranging from chicken or fish to Latin American cuisine. *Daily | Utrechtsestraat 6 | tel. 020 3 62 00 30 | www.gutsglory.nl | tram 9, 14 Rembrandtplein*

### HOTEL DE GOUDFAZANT
### (133 D2) *(ЫФ K2)*

Trendy restaurant in an industrial district in Noord. French-influenced Dutch dishes are served beneath a huge chandelier in an unadorned warehouse atmosphere. *Closed Mon | Aambeeldstraat 10h | tel. 020 6 36 5170 | bus 38 Hamerstraat*

### INSIDER TIP ▸ DE KAS ◈ (0) *(ЫФ K7)*

Organic vegetables from the restaurant's own garden are served in an 8-metre (26 ft.) tall greenhouse. The latest in Dutch food presented in an unusual atmosphere. Book ahead if you want to come in the evening! *Closed Sun | Kamerlingh Onneslaan 3 | tel. 020 4 62 45 62 | tram 9 Hoogweg*

### PONT 13 ★ (0) *(ЫФ 0)*

A converted IJ ferry, now a bit off the beaten track in the timber dock, offers a terrific atmosphere and really good food. The fish soup with rouille is excellent. *Haparandadam 50 | tel. 020 7 70 27 22 | www.pont13.nl | bus 48 Oostzaanstraat*

### & SAMHOUD PLACES (129 E2) *(ЫФ H3)*

Although the name of this restaurant is somewhat unusual, Moshik Roth's first-rate kitchen has been awarded two Michelin stars. For a fine dining experience (approx. 150 euros per person or more) head upstairs or check out the street food offered on the ground floor. *Closed Mon/Tue | Oosterdokskade 5 | tel. 020 2 60 20 94 | www.samhoudplaces.com | 5 min. walk from the main station*

Organic food in a greenhouse: De Kas

### DE SILVEREN SPIEGEL (128 B1) *(ЫФ G3)*

Atmospheric restaurant in a crooked old house dating from 1614. The emphasis is on regional products and contemporary interpretations of Dutch dishes. *Closed Sun | Kattengat 4–6 | tel. 020 6 24 65 89 | tram 1, 2, 5, 13, 17 Nieuwezijds Kolk*

### VAN VLAANDEREN (136 B2) *(ЫФ G6)*

French cuisine worthy of its star served in a friendly atmosphere. *Closed Sun–Mon | Weteringsschans 175 | tel. 020 6 22 82 92 | tram 1, 2, 5 Spui*

### D'VIJFF VLIEGHEN
(128 A4) (*m F4*)

Wooden genever barrels, Rembrandt etchings and a collection of old weapons create an authentic mood in these five 17th-century houses. The menu also upholds Dutch traditions. *Daily | Spuistraat 294–302 | tel. 020 5 30 40 60 | tram 1, 2, 5 Spui*

### YAMAZOTO (136 B4) (*m F7*)

Nothing is missing in the restaurant of the Japanese Okura Hotel, including waitresses in kimonos and a fish pond. The sashimi is served on ice, the beef raw with a hot griddle. *Daily | Ferdinand Bolstraat 333 | tel. 020 6 78 83 51 | tram 12 Cornelis Troostplein*

**RESTAURANTS: MODERATE**

### ADAM & SIAM (128 B4) (*m F4*)

Are you having trouble deciding whether you want to go for Dutch or Thai food? You can find both worlds at this bistro located in an old tobacco warehouse. The menu features rib-eye steak with roasted pumpkin alongside green beef curry with coconut milk. *Daily | Rokin 93 | tel. 020 7 77 00 80 | tram 4, 9, 14, 16 Spui*

### BLAUW ★ (134 C3) (*m C6*)

Many restaurants in Amsterdam offer "Rijstafel" featuring an array of Indonesian dishes, but most are not as authentic as the banquet offered here. I

# FAVOURITE EATERIES

### The Craft of Cooking

Whoever dines at *De Culinaire Werkplaats* **(130 C2)** (*m E2*) *(Thu–Sat evenings | Fannius Scholtenstraat 10 | tel. 06 54 64 65 76 | www.deculinairewerkplaats. nl | tram 10 Van Limburg Stirumstraat)* run by the designers Marjolein Wintjes and Eric Meursing becomes part of a masterpiece. Guest are served "eatable stories" with topics such as sincerity, time or emotions. When it comes time to pay, each patron decides what the meal was worth.

### Food Recycling

Eating what others throw out is the concept at *Instock* **(132 C5)** (*m K4*) *(daily | Czaar Peterstraat 21 | tel. 020 3 63 57 65 | www.instock.nl | tram 10 Eerste Coehoornstraat)*. 80 per cent of the ingredients used are products that were sorted out at the supermarket, such as crooked cucumbers or oranges from ripped net bags (don't worry, nothing is over the expiry date!) A new set 3 or 4 course menu is offered each day. "Rubbish" has never tasted so good!

### Dining on Board

You can enjoy a boat trip and an evening meal all in one on the tiny *Vuurtoreneiland* **(0)** (*m 0*) *(departs Wed–Sat 6:30pm, Sun 3:30pm | in front of Lloyd Hotel | Oostelijke Handelskade 34 | tram 26 Rietlandpark | www.vuurtoreneiland. nl)* in the IJsselmeer. Dine in a glass house during the summer or in an old military fort when the weather turns cold. The entire 5-course meal is prepared over an open fire or in a smoker oven because there is no electricity on the island. You must make reservations online in advance! This culinary outing takes about 5 hours, including the 40-minute boat trip each way, and costs 65 euros (beverages not included).

you think you're up for it, try Indonesia's spiciest sambal. *Daily.* | *Amstelveenseweg 158–160* | *tel. 020 6 75 50 00* | *tram 2 Amstelveenseweg*

### CAFÉ DE PONT ☆ (132 A3) *(ⓜ H2)*

This simple and likeable restaurant is right next to the quay for the IJ ferry. In summer you can sit outside with a nice view across the water. Changing daily menu, good tapas at a reasonable price. *Daily* | *Buiksloterweg 3–5* | *tel. 020 6 36 33 88* | *free ferry to Buiksloterwegveer (leaves behind the station)*

### L'ENTRECÔTE ET LES DAMES
(135 E3) *(ⓜ E6)*

This bistro is always packed before and after concerts in the nearby Concertgebouw. It won't take you long to decide what to order because there is only one starter, a salad with walnuts, which is followed by either Entrecôte or sole with fries. When it comes to dessert, however, you can choose between ten tempting French classics. *Closed Sun* | *no reservations* | *Van Baerlestraat 47–49* | *www.entrecote-et-les-dames.nl* | *tram 3, 5, 12, 16, 24 Museumplein*

### FIFTEEN (132 C4) *(ⓜ J3)*

Jamie Oliver has opened a branch of his restaurant *Fifteen* in Amsterdam. Most dishes on the menu are made with local products such as Dutch lamb, North Sea rays and blue cheese from Alkmaar. Don't expect to see Jamie himself, but at least the recipes are his. *Daily* | *Jollemanhof 9* | *tel. 020 5 09 50 15* | *tram 26 Kattenburgerstraat*

### INSIDER TIP ▶ GARTINE ◎
(128 B5) *(ⓜ F4)*

This breakfast and lunch restaurant hides in a side street off Kalverstraat. The owners serve produce from their

Vegetarian treat at Fifteen

own vegetable garden and regional products in their dishes ranging from beef salad with roast pumpkin to sausage made from Beemsterland pork. *Wed–Sun 10am–6pm* | *Taksteeg 7* | *tel. 020 3 20 41 32* | *tram 4, 9, 14, 16, 24 Spui*

### GOLDEN TEMPLE ◎ (136 B2) *(ⓜ G5)*

This vegetarian eatery mixes its styles: Indian, Arab and Mexican dishes can all be had. No smoking, no meat, no alcohol – nothing at all to harm your health. It is run by Sikhs, who are pleased to cater for vegans. *Daily* | *Utrechtsestraat 126* | *tel. 020 6 26 85 60* | *tram 4, 7, 10 Frederiksplein*

### DE GOUDEN REAEL (131 E2) *(ⓜ F1)*

Rustic French cooking in a 17th-century building. The oven-roasted leg of lamb is a treat. *Closed Mon* | *Zandhoek 14* | *tel. 020 6 23 38 83* | *bus 28 Barentszplein*

**HAPPYHAPPYJOYJOY** (133 D4) *(⬤ K3)*
The brightly-coloured pop interior is the perfect backdrop for Asian street food. Eat your way through Thai, Vietnamese, Indonesian and Chinese specialities, plus try an ice-cold Asian beer. *Daily | Oostelijke Handelskade 4 | tel. 020 3 44 64 33 | tram 26 Rietlandpark*

**HOI TIN** ★ (129 D3) *(⬤ G3)*
A big restaurant in Chinatown. At lunchtime you sit among Chinese families who enjoy a proper feast. The menu doesn't pander to European tastes, but has a range of authentic specialities. Good selection of dim sum. *Daily | Zeedijk 122–124 | tel. 020 6 25 64 51 | metro Nieuwmarkt*

**JAPANESE PANCAKE WORLD**
(131 D4) *(⬤ E3)*
And you thought pancakes were a Dutch speciality! Think again – they are a popular form of fast food in Japan. In this restaurant not far from Westermarkt, you can watch as calorie-rich Asian pancakes are conjured up in front of your eyes. *Closed Mon | Tweede Egelantiersdwarsstraat 24a | tel. 020 3 20 44 47 | www.japanesepancakeworld.com | tram 13, 14, 17 Westermarkt*

**LIEVE** (128 A2) *(⬤ F3)*
If there is one thing the Dutch appreciate about the Belgians, it is their cooking – come to Lieve to find out why. The tasting menu of Belgian beer goes well with venison paté or monkfish. *Daily | Herengracht 88 | tel. 020 6 24 96 35 | tram 13, 14, 17 Raadhuisstraat*

**L. T. CORNELIS** (131 E5–6) *(⬤ F4)*
Like the 17th-century portraits hanging on the walls, the food here takes up with Dutch traditions, but adds a decidedly modern twist. *Daily | Voetboogstraat 13 | tel. 020 2 61 48 63 | tram 4, 5, 9, 14 Spui*

**MOEDERS** ★ (131 D5) *(⬤ E4)*
Home food just the way mum cooks – and that is why the walls here are covered with hundreds of photos of mothers. The menu is traditionally Dutch, but there are a few dishes that might have been rustled up by a Mediterranean mamma. *Daily | Rozengracht 251 | tel. 020 6 26 79 57 | tram 10, 13, 14, 17 Marnixstraat or Rozengracht*

**NEW KING** (129 D3) *(⬤ G3)*
A Chinese restaurant with a dim interior that is always bursting at the seams. Chinese classics, but also some rare dishes ranging from aubergine with tofu to stuffed squid. *Daily. | Zeedijk 115–117 | tel. 020 6 25 21 80 | metro Nieuwmarkt*

**PATA NEGRA** ★ (136 B1) *(⬤ G5)*
Spain in Amsterdam: walk through the door of this noisy and always crowded tapas restaurant and you'll think you've been beamed to Seville. Beneath the hams hanging from the ceiling are simple wooden benches, the wine is served in ceramic jugs. *Daily | Utrechtsestraat 124 | tel. 020 4 22 62 50 | tram 4 Prinsengracht*

**DE PLANTAGE** ★ (132 B6) *(⬤ H4)*
Eat with the flamingos! Don't worry, they won't appear on your plate. In the loveliest conservatory in Amsterdam, modern bistro-style food is served up on the large ⬥ patio during the summer, where you can enjoy the view of the flamingos and spoonbills. *Daily | Plantage Kerklaan 36 | tel. 020 7 60 86 00 | tram 9, 14 Artis*

**INSIDER TIP** ▶ **REM EILAND** ⬥ (0) *(⬤ 0)*
In the 1960s, this slightly odd tower construction, now in the old wood harbour (Oude Houthaven), stood in the North Sea and housed a pirate transmitter, later a water measurement station. In 2011 it was relocated to the wood harbour and converted into a restaurant with a pano-

Authentic tapas restaurant in the heart of Amsterdam: Pata Negra

ramic view. The kitchen serves up modern Dutch and Mediterranean cuisine. *Daily | Haparandadam 45 | tel. 020 6 88 55 01 | bus 22, 48 Oostzaanstraat*

**INSIDER TIP RIJSEL** (137 D4) *(ﾉﾉ H7)*

Rijsel is the Flemish name of the northern French city of Lillet whose rustic charm infuses this rotisserie restaurant. Simple, yet perfectly prepared dishes ranging from Breton fish soup to Côte de Boeuf with baked potatoes. *Closed Sun/Mon | Marcusstraat 52b | tel. 020 4 63 21 42 | www.rijsel.com | metro Wibautstraat*

**DE ROZENBOOM** (128 B5) *(ﾉﾉ E4)*

This tiny restaurant with its antique Dutch interior has a menu to match its ambience. Choose from among pancakes, soups, *stamppot* and other classic Dutch dishes. *Closed Sun | Rozenboomsteeg 6 | tel. 020 6 22 50 24 | tram 1, 2, 5 Spui*

**SAMBA KITCHEN** (136 A3) *(ﾉﾉ F7)*

See if you can still do the samba after this Brazilian treat: for a fixed price of 27.50 euros you eat as much grilled and marinated meat, plus side dishes, as you want. *Daily | Ceintuurbaan 63 | tel. 020 6 76 05 13 | tram 3, 12 Ferdinand Bolstraat*

**DE STRUISVOGEL** ⊗ (131 D5) *(ﾉﾉ F4)*

Cosy cellar with good bistro food. Various three-course menus for 25 euros, all the meat is organic. *Daily | Keizersgracht 312 | tel. 020 4 23 38 17 | tram 13, 14, 17 Westermarkt*

**WORST** (131 E1) *(ﾉﾉ F1)*

Homemade sausages and wine steal the show at this bar. The guests sitting

With all the colour of the Bazar around you, it has to be oriental food

on stools around large tables can keep an eye on the chefs cooking away in the open kitchen. *Closed Mon | Barentsz-straat 171 | tel. 020 6 25 61 67 | deworst. nl | tram 3 Zoutkeetsgracht*

## RESTAURANTS: BUDGET

### BAZAR (136 B3) (*⊞ G6*)
Oriental restaurant on Albert Cuypmarkt, furnished with lots of Arabian kitsch. A big, noisy place with a cheerful atmosphere where you can get an oriental breakfast from 11am. *Daily | Albert Cuypstraat 182 | tel. 020 6 75 05 44 | tram 16, 24 Albert Cuypstraat*

### BIRD (129 D2) (*⊞ G3*)
Pictures of Thailand's king and queen decorate the walls while the sound system blares Asian pop music. This takeaway is colourful, unique and anything but quiet. Don't confuse it with the more expensive restaurant of the same name across the way! *Daily | Zeedijk 77 | tel. 020 4 20 62 89 | metro Nieuwmarkt*

### BURGERMEESTER (128 C6) (*⊞ F4*)
This small restaurant chain offers juicy burgers of all kinds, served just as you like it: rare, medium or well done. No reservations! *Daily | Utrechtsestraat 8 | tram 4, 9 Rembrandtplein*

### FOU FOW RAMEN (131 D5) (*⊞ E4*)
Large bowls filled with steaming hot Japanese noodle soups, with or without meat or chili, served with homemade gyoza dumplings. An ideal way to boost your energy for some more shopping. *Closed Mon | Elandsgracht 2a | tram 7, 10 Elandsgracht*

**KADIJK** (129 F4) *(ᗰ H4)*
It looks like a normal café on the outside, but Indonesian specialities are served inside. Delicious mackerel. *Daily | Kadijkplein 5 | tel. 020 1 77 44 41 | 10 min. walk from the main station*

**NAM KEE** (129 D3) *(ᗰ G3)*
The Dutch hit film "The Oysters of Nam Kee" made this Chinese restaurant a legend. Simple and reasonably-priced food, tasty noodle soup and efficient but not so friendly service. *Daily | Zeedijk 111 –113 | tel. 020 6 24 34 07 | metro Nieuwmarkt*

**PALOMA BLANCA** (134 C1) *(ᗰ D5)*
Sweet peppermint tea and delicious couscous, if no alcohol, are on offer at this Moroccan restaurant. *Closed Mon | Jan Pieter Heijestraat 145 | tel. 020 7 71 46 06 | tram 7, 10 Jan Pieter Heijestraat*

**INSIDER TIP PANCAKES!** (131 D5) *(ᗰ F4)*
A tiny pancake restaurant in a shopping street. Deliciously thin pancakes and a child-friendly environment. No reservations! *Daily | Berenstraat 38 | tram 13, 14, 17 Westermarkt*

**SARAVANAA BHAVAN** (136 B2) *(ᗰ G6)*
Who would have thought that you could feel like you are in India in the heart of Amsterdam? This Indian restaurant is large, loud and always crowded. Dishes are served in authentic aluminium bowls. Since you probably won't know even half of what is listed on the menu, you'll just have to take your chances and try a few things. *Daily | Stadhouderskade 123 | tel. 020 7 53 12 50 | tram 4 Stadhouderskade*

**THE SEAFOOD BAR** ⓦ (135 E2) *(ᗰ E5)*
In this fish restaurant near Museumplein you can order a three course meal as well as fish & chips and snacks – everything is fresh off the boat or from sustainable breeding and fisheries. No reservations! *Daily | Van Baerlestraat 5 | tram 2, 3, 5, 12 Van Baerlestraat*

**SEMHAR** (130 C4) *(ᗰ E3)*
Spicy Ethiopian dishes that you scoop up with a piece of pancake instead of a knife and fork. Try a glass of banana beer or **INSIDER TIP** mocha with incense. *Daily | Marnixstraat 259–261 | tel. 020 6 38 16 34 | tram 10 Bloemgracht*

**WARUNG MARLON** (136 B3) *(ᗰ F6)*
Surinamese snack bar on Albert Cuypmarkt serving up its popular *saoto soup* (chicken broth with lemongrass and egg) and fried bananas. *Daily | Eerste Van der Helststraat 55 | no reservations | tram 16, 24 Albert Cuypstraat*

## LOW BUDGET

A street stall called *Vlaams Friethuis Vleminckx* **(128 B5)** *(ᗰ E4)* (*Daily | Voetboogstraat 31 | tram 1, 2, 5 Koningsplein*) sells the best French fries in all Amsterdam, which is why there is often a long queue. Choose between 20 (!) kinds of mayonnaise.

Surinamese breadrolls are exotic, delicious and affordable. *Tjin's* **(136 C2)** *(ᗰ G6)* (*daily | Van Woustraat 17 | tram 4 Stadhouderskade*) offers food starting at 4 euros, for example a sandwich topped with pickled beef and stringbeans.

Arabian chickpea balls in pita bread, and as much as you want from the salad buffet, that's the deal at *Maoz Falafel* **(128 B5)** *(ᗰ G4)* (*daily | Muntplein 1 | tram 4, 9, 16, 24 Muntplein*). Additional locations: *Leidsestraat 85* and *Damrak 40*

# SHOPPING

Amsterdam's most typical shopping area is **9 straatjes (131 D–E5)** (*E–F4*), nine little streets that run from west to east between Westermarkt and Leidsegracht: Reestraat, Runstraat, Berenstraat and their continuations. There are loads of little shops with big selections, ranging from designer fashion to art books, from junk to Dutch cheese – and lots of nice cafés. The nearest tram stops for the *9 straatjes* are Westermarkt (tram 13, 14, 17), Dam (tram 1, 2, 5, 13, 14, 17) and Spui (tram 1, 2, 5).

Amsterdam is a wonderland for shoppers. The shops in the city centre are open on Sundays, and the sales assistants are astonishingly friendly even when it's really hectic.

The epicentre of the shopping action is the triangle formed by Dam, Muntplein and Leidseplein. In the Kalvertoren and ● *Magna Plaza* shopping centres, you can hunt bargains in comfort even when it rains. But what really makes Amsterdam attractive to shoppers are all the little stores known as *winkels* in Dutch that are not part of any chain stores. There is a diverse mix of these shops and pleasant cafés in the *9 straatjes* as well as in Utrechtsestraat and on the Haarlemmerdijk Around Museumplein, especially in P. C

## *Winkelen* in shopping heaven: Plenty of little shops make Amsterdam a mecca for shopaholics and collectors

Hooftstraat, you will find the high-end addresses as international designer labels and luxury boutiques have moved in here. Locals often buy their everyday items and groceries at the markets, especially Albert Cuypmarkt, where you can surely find something nice to take home.

The international flavour of Amsterdam is apparent in the ● *tokos,* exotic little shops selling Thai, Surinamese and Indian food, which can also be found close to Albert Cuypmarkt.

ANTIQUES

**EDUARD KRAMER** (136 A1) *(⑫ F5)*
Antique Dutch tiles in every price range, from Baroque to Art Nouveau, from blue-and-white to colourful. *Nieuwe Spiegelstraat 64 | www.antique-tileshop. nl | tram 16, 24 Vijzelgracht*

**DE LOOIER** (131 D5) *(⑫ E4)*
De Looier is the largest covered antiques market in the Netherlands. Its building on Lijnbaansgracht houses over 70

Where staff is busy as a bee: the classy department store De Bijenkorf

stands and several shops, though some of the stands are hardly bigger than a showcase. They sell everything from porcelain to toys and furniture. *Elandsgracht 109 | tram 7, 10, 17 Elandsgracht*

### NEEF LOUIS (0) *(𝄞 0)*
Strictly speaking, this shop situated in an old warehouse in Noord does not sell antiques, but rather vintage furniture. There are plenty of designer pieces (with a price to match) to be found among the old school desks and workshop lamps. *Papaverweg 46–48 | bus 38 Klaprozenweg*

## BOOKS

### ANTIQUATIAAT KOK ★
(128 C4) *(𝄞 G4)*
This huge antiquarian bookshop filled with treasures is a paradise for book lovers. They also stock old maps and prints some of which are matted. *Oude Hoogstraat 18 | metro Nieuwmarkt*

### ATHENAEUM (128 A5) *(𝄞 F4)*
One of the city's best-stocked bookstores and the adjoining newsagent's has a huge range of magazines. *Spui 14–16 | tram 1, 2, 5 Spui*

### BOEKENMARKT OUDEMANHUISPOORT
(128 C4–5) *(𝄞 G4)*
This book market is located well sheltered in an 18th century arcade in the university quarter. *Oudemanhuispoort | tram 4, 9, 14, 16, 24 Spui*

## EATABLES

### DE BIERKONING (128 B3) *(𝄞 F3)*
300 different beer glasses and 900 brews from all over the world to pour into them, including obscure regional beers, justify the "beer king's" name. *Paleisstraat 125 | www.bierkoning.nl | tram 1, 2, 5, 13, 14, 17 Dam*

### JACOB HOOY & CO ★
(128 C4) *(𝄞 G3)*
Entering this spice shop is like taking a trip back in time. 500 kinds of herbs and spices, stored in wooden drawers and barrels labelled in gold lettering, fill the space with their aromas. Behind the counter you see 30 jars of *drop* – salty or sweet Dutch liquorice. *Kloveniersburgwal 10–12 | metro Nieuwmarkt*

### INSIDER TIP KAASHUIS TROMP
(136 B1) *(𝄞 G5)*
Dutch and international cheese is piled to the rafters in this little shop on Utrechtsestraat. The staff is ready to help and will let you try them before you buy *Utrechtsestraat 90 | tram 4 Prinsengracht*

**MARQT** ★ ◎ (131 F6) *(ﾉﾉ G4)*
, fashionable supermarket that sells
nly eco-friendly and regional prod-
cts. Buy something to take home
uch as cheese, salty liquorice or beer
rom local breweries, or pick up a fresh
izza and salad to eat straight away.
*trechtsestraat 17 | tram 4, 9, 14 Rem-
randtplein*

**INSIDER TIP PUCCINI** (128 C5) *(ﾉﾉ G4)*
hocolate lovers will surely drool over
he selection at Puccini's. The choco-
ates are big and as unusual as they are
elicious. Try some chocolate combined
vith a scent of thyme, lemongrass or
in. *Staalstraat 17 | tram 9, 14 Water-
oplein*

## GALLERIES

**GALERIE FONS WELTERS** ●
131 D4) *(ﾉﾉ E3)*
his gallery is dedicated to contem-
orary Dutch art, much of it too big to
arry. *Bloemstraat 140 | tram 13, 14, 17
Vestermarkt*

**RON MANDOS GALERIE**
(131 D5) *(ﾉﾉ E4)*
One of the best-known galleries for
contemporary international art. It sometimes houses themed exhibits or features
shows by individual artists. *Prinsen-
gracht 282 | tram 13, 14, 17 Westermarkt*

## DEPARTMENT STORES

**BIJENKORF** ★ (128 B3) *(ﾉﾉ F3)*
The department store, founded in 1870,
is chic and expensive. Gucci and Co.
beckon on the marble-clad ground floor,
while on the upper floors you can also
find more affordable designer brands.
*Dam 1 | tram 4, 9, 16, 24 Dam*

**INSIDER TIP HEMA** (128 B5) *(ﾉﾉ F4)*
What used to be a very basic store has
become a kind of Dutch Ikea. Here you
can get goods ranging from toilet brush-
es and sofa pillows to baby jumpers with
minimalist and often amazingly good
design. *E.g. in the Kalvertoren shopping
centre (Kalverstraat | Heiligeweg | tram 4,
9, 14, 16, 24 Muntplein)*

---

★ **Antiquariaat Kok**
ots of shelves filled with books and
rints to browse through to your
eart's content → p. 70

★ **Jacob Hooy & Co**
illed with the aromas of spice and
ea → p. 70

★ **Marqt**
upermarket devoted to regional and
rganic products → p. 71

★ **Bijenkorf**
raditional department store on the
am → p. 71

★ **Albert Cuypmarkt**
Multicultural outdoor market → p. 72

★ **IJ-Hallen**
Europe's largest flea market is housed
in a former shipyard hall → p. 72

★ **Heinen Delftware**
Genuine Royal Delft and other hand-
painted porcelain → p. 74

★ **Hajenius**
This cigar smokers' paradise has
wood panelling and crystal chande-
liers → p. 75

**MARCO POLO HIGHLIGHTS**

## THIS & THAT

### KITSCH KITCHEN SUPERMERCADO
(131 D4) (*E3*)
Bright colours and crazy patterns distinguish the household items from developing countries sold here. Lovely items to take home with you. *Rozengracht 8–12 | tram 13, 14, 17 Westermarkt*

### PERFUMES OF THE PAST
(131 E3) (*F2*)
Have you been searching for the perfect scent? This tiny shop stocks just about every classic perfume. *Binnen Oraniestraat 11 | 10 min. walk from the main station*

### DE WITTE TANDEN WINKEL
(131 D5) (*F4*)
You'll find nothing but toothbrushes in this *winkel,* from unusual models for toothbrush freaks to special devices for dental hygiene. *Runstraat 5 | tram 13, 14, 17 Westermarkt*

## MARKETS

### ALBERT CUYPMARKT ★
(136 B3) (*F–G6*)
Anything and everything can be found at Amsterdam's biggest and best-known outdoor market that is truly multicultural. See, smell and buy vegetables, fish, cheese, spices and flowers, as well as Indian fabrics and African hair gel. *Mon–Sat 9:30am–5pm | tram 16, 24 Albert Cuypstraat, Stadhouderskade*

### FLOWER MARKET (128 A–B5) (*F4*)
Here they sell everything to send gardeners into a state of bliss: flower bulbs, houseplants and balcony flowers – though the prices might make you take a deep breath. *Mon–Sat 9:30am–5pm | Singel 610–616 | tram 1, 2, 4, 5 Königplein & tram 9, 14, 16, 24 Muntplein*

### IJ-HALLEN ★ (0) (*0*)
Once a month, half of Amsterdam seems to trek to the NDSM shipyard, which is

Caps, sunglasses, fabrics, fish – it's all to be had at Albert Cuypmarkt

ow home to Europe's largest flea market. The huge, impressive halls are chock ull of second-hand items. You can check ut the dates for the market online. *Sat/ un 9am–4:30pm | admission 5 euros | T Neveritaweg 1 | www.ijhallen.nl | free erry from the main station to the NDSM hipyard*

**OORDERMARKT** (131 E3) (*∭ F2*)

round the Noorderkerk there are flea market stands every Monday and organic ood is sold here on Saturdays. You can ombine a stroll along the ⬤ organic market with a visit to the food stalls on djoining Lindengracht. *Mon 9am–4pm lea market, Sat 9am–4pm organic pro- duce | Noordermarkt and Westerstraat | ram 3 Marnixplein*

**WATERLOOPLEIN** (129 D5) (*∭ G4*)

he city's only regular flea market is on Waterlooplein. It sells everything imagi- able, from bike tyres and inner tubes o incense burners and second-hand eather jackets. *Mon–Sat 10am–5pm | Waterlooplein | tram 9, 14, metro Wa- erlooplein*

## FASHION & ACCESSORIES

**IUTSPOT** (131 D5) (*∭ E4*)

f you are a fan of tight jeans, oversized oats and classic-style racing bikes, then ou will love this concept store featuring oung designer clothes and a hip café. *Rozengracht 204–210 | tram 13, 14, 17 Marnixstraat*

**NDIVIDUALS** (128 B5) (*∭ F4*)

wice a year 13 Amsterdam students of ashion design present a new collection here. Stylists and fashion editors come here in search of new talent. *Spui 23 | ram 1, 2, 4, 5, 9, 14, 16, 24 Spui*

**JAN** (131 F6) (*∭ G5*)

Designer bits and bobs, from handbags and jewellery to lifestyle books and ac- cessories for the home. *Utrechtsestraat 74 | tram 4 Keizersgracht*

**JUTKA & RISKA** (130 C5) (*∭ D4*)

A little bit out of the way, but the vintage fashion and accessories from the 1970s and 1980s plus newer items designed by sisters Jutka and Riska Volkerts' own la- bel make the trip more than worthwhile. *Bilderdijkstraat 194 | tram 3, 7, 10, 12, 14, 17 Bilderdijkstraat*

**MARLIES DEKKERS** (131 D5) (*∭ F4*)

Flagship store of the "grande dame" of fashionable Dutch underwear. Extremely sexy lingerie without frills is presented in luxurious Snow White-style surroundings. *Berenstraat 18 | tram 13, 14, 17 Wester- markt*

**NUKUHIVA** ⬤ (131 E3) (*∭ G2*)

You might not notice when you look at the jeans and basics here, but this little boutique specialises in fair-trade fashion. Some of the profits go to educational projects in the developing world. *Haar- lemmerstraat 36 | 10 min. walk from the main station*

**SISSY BOY** (133 E4) (*∭ L3*)

A Dutch fashion chain that also sells accessories for the home. Come here for wearable clothes and basics or beautiful scarves made by *Jago*. *KNSM- laan 19 | tram 10 Azartplein*

**SPRMRKT** (131 D5) (*∭ E4*)

New designer fashion, used designer furniture and all kinds of trendy accesso- ries in a barn-like store on Rozengracht. *Rozengracht 191–193 | tram 13, 14, 17 Marnixstraat*

## X BANK

(128 A3) *(Ⓜ F3)*

The 700 m² (7,535 sq. ft.) shop on the mezzanine floor of the W Hotel is bursting at the seams with Dutch design. Fashion, art, and accessories are sorted by colour like a rainbow. Nothing is cheap, but you can browse for hours. *Spui-straat 172 | tram 1, 2, 5, 13, 14, 17 Dam*

**INSIDERTIP YDU – YOUNG DESIGNERS UNITED**

(131 E6) *(Ⓜ F4)*

Unknown young designers can rent space on the racks here to sell their creative work. They guarantee that there are no more than four of each piece. *Keizersgracht 447 | tram 1, 2, 5 Keizersgracht*

## LOW BUDGET

For lower prices and fewer crowds, but just as much variety as Albert Cuypmarkt, go to the *Dappermarkt* **(137 E1)** *(Ⓜ K5)* (Mon–Sat 10am–4:30pm | Dapperstraat | tram 14 Pontanusstraat & tram 9 1e from Swindenstraat)* in the trendy Oost quarter.

In Dutch supermarkets *exotic spices* are much cheaper than elsewhere in Europe. As Indonesia was once a Dutch colony, the choice is enormous – from dried lemongrass to cumin and fenugreek.

Buy flowers and flower bulbs on the street markets that sell food! They cost half as much as at the flower market on Singel!

## JEWELLERY & DIAMONDS

**GASSAN DAM SQUARE** (128 B3) *(Ⓜ F3)*
Just pop in and buy some precious stones at this big diamond dealer located right on the Dam. Apart from sparkling gem stones you can pick up a high-end wrist watch. *Rokin 1–5 | tram 4, 9, 16, 24 Dam*

**LIJFERING & ROS** (128 C4) *(Ⓜ G4)*
Paul Lijfering and Angelique Ros lovingly restore and sell Art Nouveau jewellery and old watches. *Oudemanhuispoort 1a | tram 9, 14, 16, 24 Spui*

## SHOES

**INSIDERTIP OTTEN & ZOON**
(136 B3) *(Ⓜ F6)*
Since 1898 this shop in a side street off Albert Cuypmarkt has sold genuine clogs and other orthopaedic shoes, and definitely not at tourist prices. *1e van de Helststraat 31 | tram 16, 24 Albert Cuyp markt*

**SHOEBALOO**
(128 A5) *(Ⓜ F4)*
The gleaming white interior of this shop is futuristic and spacey. It is stocked with shoes from luxury brands such as Prada. *Koningsplein 5 | tram 1, 2, 5 Koningsplein*

**INSIDERTIP UNITED NUDE**
(128 A4) *(Ⓜ F4)*
Dutch shoe design with a flair for eye catching heels by the nephew of the famous architect Rem Koolhaas. *Spui straat 125a | tram 1, 2, 5 Spui*

## SOUVENIRS

**HEINEN DELFTWARE** ★
(135 F1) *(Ⓜ F3)*
Father Jaap and son Joris paint some of the porcelain themselves, but also sel

products from the Royal Delft porcelain manufactory. *Prinsengracht 440 | tram 3, 14, 17 Westermarkt*

## THINKING OF HOLLAND
(132 B4) (*∅ J3*)

A souvenir shop without clogs or tulips, but rather original items by Dutch designers to wear or display, ranging in price from cheap to high-end. *Piet Heinkade 23 (in the cruise ship terminal) | tram 26 Muziekgebouw*

## TOBACCO

### HAJENIUS ★
(128 B4) (*∅ F4*)

Tobacco, cigarettes and hand-rolled cigars have been sold since 1826 in the elegant Empire interior of this long-established tobacconist's shop with its wood panelling and crystal chandeliers. *Rokin 92 | tram 4, 9, 14, 16, 24 Spui*

## DESIGN FOR THE HOME

### DROOG@HOME (128 C5) (*∅ G4*)

In the mid-1990s Droog Design made a name for itself with an experimental look. A few years ago, the designers' collective set up its own shop and gallery. *Staalstraat 7b | tram 9, 14 Waterlooplein*

### INSIDER TIP FROZEN FOUNTAIN
(131 D6) (*∅ F4*)

Unconventional forms for everything from chairs to lamps. Nothing is off the peg, and that has its price. *Prinsengracht 645 | tram 7, 10 Raamplein*

### WAAR ✪ (130 C5) (*∅ D4*)

Fair-trade shop with an emphasis on design. At Waar you can buy not only fair-trade food but also crockery, vases, baskets and bathroom accessories with a modern and minimalist style. *Bilderdijkstraat 57 | tram 3, 12, 13, 14, 17 Bilderdijkstraat*

Encounters of the third kind at Frozen Fountain

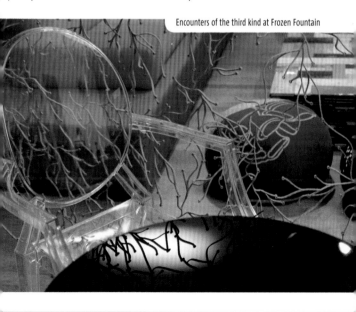

# ENTERTAINMENT

**CITY WHERE TO START?**
Amsterdam's **Leidseplein (131 D6)** *(🗺 E5)* is the beating heart of entertainment in Amsterdam. In the evening, this rather chaotic square bursts with life in its pubs, cinemas, theatres and clubs. The Stadsschouwburg, Kino City and the De Balie arts centre stand directly on the square. Clubs such as Jimmy Woo and Sugar Factory are hidden away in the narrow streets around Leidseplein, and Paradiso and Melkweg are not far away at all. The best way to get there is by tram. Routes 1, 2, 3, 5, 7 and 10 stop at Leidseplein.

Amsterdam never seems to sleep, especially at weekends. The city centre is abuzz all night long as taxis and cyclists jam the narrow streets, and in summer the countless outdoor cafés are packed. The hotspots for nightlife are Leidseplein and Rembrandtplein. Around Spui and Nieuwmarkt and in the De Pijp quarter the action is less touristy.

The traditional way to kick off the evening is *borreluur*, which is an after-office rendezvous when colleagues meet in one of the "brown cafés", i.e. a wood-panelled pub, for beer and snacks. A host of theatres offer a good dose of culture, though most performances are in Dutch. For an evening out without a language barrier, visitors can attend performances by famous Dutch dance

Borreluur, music and canal trips: there's almost more going on in the city centre after dark than during the day

and music ensembles such as the *Concertgebouw Orchestra* or *Nederlands Dans Theater*. Make your booking in good time, as tickets are seldom available at the last minute. For information, advance sales and reservations go to the *Amsterdam Uitbureau* in the Stadsschouwburg *(see p. 83)*.

For music at higher decibels, head to the clubs and concert halls. Just about every genre from house to soul can be found in the city, either in cosy living room clubs or mega venue spaces.

## BARS

**APT.** (128 A5) *(ⅅ F4)*
This small but trendy cocktail bar shares the historic Odeon building on Singel with the pub *Hoppa* and the legendary *Supperclub*. Drinks are shaken until the early hours. *Sun–Wed 7pm–2am, Thu–Sat 7pm–4am | Singel 460 | tram 1, 2, 5 Koningsplein*

**MADAM** ☆ (132 A2) *(ⅅ G2)*
High up in the A'DAM tower, you can enjoy the best view of the city, accom-

Try them all: over 200 kinds of beer at In de Wildeman

## CAFÉS & PUBS

During the week most cafés and pubs are open until 1am, at weekends they stay open two hours longer.

### BROUWERIJ 'T IJ ⚫ (133 F6) (*ᗯ K4*)

One of Amsterdam's few beer gardens is next to a historic windmill. The mill is home to the local t'IJ brewery, which makes 100% organic, unfiltered beer *Daily | Funenkade 7 | tram 10 Hoogte Kadijk & tram 14 Pontanusstraat*

### DE CEUVEL ⚫ (0) (*ᗯ 0*)

Dry-docked houseboats in the old ship yard serve as offices for creative businesses. The café was furnished entirely from second-hand materials. It offers organic food and local beers, attracting a young and alternative crowd, especially in summer. *Sun, Tue, Wed, Thu 11am–midnight Fri/Sat 11am–2am | Korte Papaverweg 4 | bus 31, 34, 391, 394 Mosplein*

### DE OOSTERLING ⚫

(136 B2) (*ᗯ G5*)

Traditional pub with genuine Amsterdam regulars, family-run for 100 years. Rustic wooden fittings, a good range of beers no music. *Utrechtsestraat 140 | tram 4, 7, 10 Frederiksplein*

panied by cocktails and club music. *Daily after 9pm (opens as a restaurant earlier) | Overhoeksplein 3 | free ferry from the main station to Buiksloterweg*

### NOL (131 D3) (*ᗯ F3*)

A genuine Jordaan bar with flowered wallpaper and crystal chandeliers. The regulars often sing along to Dutch hits played by the band. *Westerstraat 109 | tram 3 Marnixplein*

### POREM (129 D2) (*ᗯ G3*)

Don't hesitate to ring the bell at this hidden speakeasy on the edge of the red light district. Sushi, Dim Sum and delicious cocktails await inside. *Mon–Thu 6pm–1am, Fri/Sat 6pm–3am | Geldersekade 17 | 5 min. walk from the main station*

### VYNE (131 D5) (*ᗯ F4*)

Wine is what it's all about here. Refrigerators full of bottles line the entire left hand side of the room. *Prinsengracht 411 | tram 13, 14, 17 Westermarkt*

### IN DE WILDEMAN ★

(128 C2) (*ᗯ G3*)

This *proeflokaal* in an old distillery looks like a cross between a pub and an old fashioned pharmacy. Over 200 kinds of beer, 17 of them on draught. *Closed Sun | Kolksteeg 3 | tram 1, 2, 5 Kolk*

# ENTERTAINMENT

## INSIDER TIP WYNAND FOCKINK ●
(128 B3) (*Ш G4*)

A tiny *proeflokaal* ("tasting room") dating from 1679 in a covered alleyway near the Krasnapolsky Hotel. A distillery that makes 60 kinds of schnapps is located behind it. Closes at 9pm! *Pijlsteeg 1 | tram 4, 9, 16, 24 Dam*

## CLUBS & DISCOS

Amsterdam has a fairly laid-back clubbing scene: dress codes hardly exist, and the guys on the door are generally not a real problem, although you do sometimes have to wait patiently to get in.

### BITTERZOET (128 B1) (*Ш G3*)

If you have had enough techno music and electro beats, then *Bitterzoet* is the right place. Dance the night away to the friendly sounds of jazz, soul and funk. Concerts are often held during the week. *Admission 10 euros | Spuistraat 2 | www.bitterzoet.com | 5 min. walk from the main station*

### CLUB AIR (128 G6) (*Ш C4*)

A big club with electronic beats of the experimental kind. A prepaid system simplifies paying at the bar. *Amstelstraat 16 | www.air.nl | tram 4, 9, 14 Rembrandtplein*

### ESCAPE (128 C6) (*Ш G4*)

One of the city's biggest clubs, accommodating up to 2,500 guests. Be prepared to queue at weekends, and when you get to the door there's no guarantee they'll let you in. *Admission from 12 euros | Rembrandtplein 11–15 | www.escape.nl | tram 4 Rembrandtplein*

### JIMMY WOO ★ (135 F1) (*Ш E5*)

Cool location with a Chinese touch. Beneath more than 12,000 lamps, Amsterdam's young and beautiful crowd groove to house music on an enormous dance floor. You can chill out on black leather sofas between Asian antiques in the lounge. *Admission from 10 euros | Korte Leidsedwarsstraat 18 | www.jimmywoo.com | tram 1, 2, 5, 7, 10 Leidseplein*

---

★ **In de Wildeman**
A choice made difficult: in this ancient *proeflokaal* (tasting room) you can try 200 kinds of beer → p. 78

★ **Jimmy Woo**
A Chinese-style star in the Amsterdam night sky → p. 79

★ **Paradiso**
Pop, rock and techno where hymns were once sung → p. 80

★ **Canal trips**
A true Amsterdam experience: glide along canals after dark → p. 80

★ **Tuschinski**
A fabulous old cinema – inside and out → p. 82

★ **Concertgebouw**
One of the world's top orchestras benefits from superb acoustics → p. 82

★ **Het Muziektheater**
Something for every mood from experimental dance to grand opera → p. 83

★ **Stadsschouwburg**
Theatre on Leidseplein with an extensive programme → p. 83

MARCO POLO HIGHLIGHTS

## MELKWEG (135 F1) (*∭ E5*)

Legendary arts centre in a converted dairy with a changing programme of concerts, disco, films and exhibitions. *Café from 1pm, meals 6pm–9pm | admission 4–15 euros depending on event | Lijnbaansgracht 234 | www.melkweg.nl | tram 1, 2, 5, 7, 10 Leidseplein*

## PARADISO ★ (135 F1) (*∭ F5*)

This legendary dance club and stage for concerts housed in a converted church has been a fixture in the nightlife of Amsterdam since the days of punk. Changing programme of events and techno DJs at weekends. *Admission up to 20 euros | Weteringschans 6–8 | www.paradiso.nl | tram 1, 2, 5, 7, 10 Leidseplein*

## SHELTER (132 A2) (*∭ G2*)

This is an underground club in the truest sense of the word. Located in the basement of the A'DAM tower, its underground entrance is not opened until after sundown. The DJs play all kinds of techno music. *Fri/Sat from 11pm | admission from 10 euros | Overhoeksplein 1 | free ferry from the main station to Buiksloterweg*

## SUGAR FACTORY (135 F1) (*∭ E5*)

A small all-round club that is a venue for DJ sets but also hosts theatre productions and art performances. The musical offerings range from electro to jazz and world music. *Admission from 8.50 euros | Lijnbaansgracht 238 | www.sugarfactory.nl | tram 1, 2, 5, 7, 10 Leidseplein*

## WESTERUNIE (130 C2) (*∭ D1*)

Every weekend Dutch DJs do their stuff in a hall of the old Westergasfabrik (gas works). The huge, 12-metre-high (39 ft.) hall holds up to 800 revellers. *Klönneplein 4 | www.westerunie.nl | tram 10 Van Hallstraat*

### CANAL TRIPS

★ Glide along the canals at night – what could be more romantic? The boats operated by *Rederij Lovers (daily, every half hour between 6pm and 10pm | 16 euros | Prins Hendrikkade 25–27, opposite the main station | tel. 020 5 30 10 90)* spends an hour passing illuminated bridges and the façades of canal-side houses in the historic quarter. Here and there you get a glimpse of the scene inside a lit-up houseboat.

If you'd like to have something to eat on the boat, why not go on a *Cheese and Wine Cruise (daily 8:30pm | 37.50 euros including wine and cheese | departure from the Gray Line pier, Prins Hendrikkade 33a | www.stromma.nl)* with *Canal Company*.

## JAZZ CLUBS

**BIMHUIS** (132 B3) *(ⓜ H3)*

Internationally renowned jazz venue, founded in 1974 and now housed in a spectacular new waterfront building. Mon–Wed jam sessions from 10pm. *Closed July and Aug | Piet Heinkade 3 | Tel. 020 788 2188 | 5 min. walk from the main station*

**CASABLANCA** (129 D2) *(ⓜ G3)*

The oldest and probably the most famous jazz club in the Netherlands. Back in 1945 the war generation danced to the sounds of Kit Dynamite and other jazz greats of the era. "Open Podium" on Saturdays and Sundays. *Zeedijk 26 | 5 min. walk from the main station*

**NORTH SEA JAZZ CLUB**

130 C2) *(ⓜ D1)*

Amsterdam's answer to the Blue Note Club in New York. While your ears take in the wonderful sounds of jazz, funk, soul and world music, your taste buds will delight in the yummy cocktails from *Billie's Bar. Daily from 7pm, concerts begin at 9pm | Pazzanistraat 1 | tram 10 Westerpark*

## CASINO

**HOLLAND CASINO**

(135 F1) *(ⓜ E5)*

A striking round building is home to one of Europe's most modern casinos. If you are over 18 and properly dressed, you can play roulette, blackjack, poker, etc. beneath a colourful glass dome. *Admission 5 euros | Max Euweplein 62 | tram 1, 2, 5, 7, 10 Leidseplein*

## CINEMAS

All films are shown in the original language with Dutch subtitles. Evening screenings usually start at 8pm and 10pm. Some cinemas interrupt the movie for a ten-minute break.

Do good dancers go to heaven? Club Paradiso occupies a former church

INSIDER TIP **THE MOVIES** ●
(131 D2) (𝄞 F2)

Smaller than the Tuschinski and not as well known, but almost equally beautiful: Amsterdam's oldest cinema on Haarlemmerdijk was opened in 1912. The auditorium and café-restaurant have Art Deco interiors. *Haarlemmerdijk 161 | tel. 020 6 38 60 16 | tram 3 Haarlemmerplein*

### TUSCHINSKI ★
(128 B6) (𝄞 G4)

When the King's mother Beatrix feels like going to the cinema, she selects the Tuschinski. And she knows why – it's a right royal treat because this movie palace built in 1921 is an Expressionist architectural gem. Take a seat in its great auditorium or stroll through the foyer, and you will feel like you hav● been transported back in time. *Regulie● breestraat 26 | tel. 0900 14 58 | tram 4, 14 Rembrandtplein*

## CONCERTS & BALLET

### CONCERTGEBOUW ★
(135 E3) (𝄞 E6)

Amsterdam's concert hall is a legen● and so are its acoustics. In the box-lik● main hall with its restrained decoratio● you can really hear a pin drop on th● stage.

The Concertgebouworkest of the Dutc● capital is one of the world's finest orche● tras. *Concertgebouwplein 10 | tel. 090● 6 71 83 45 | www.concertgebouw.nl | tra● 3, 5, 12, 16 Museumplein*

# FOR BOOKWORMS AND FILM BUFFS

**The Miniaturist** – The young Nella marries a rich merchant and moves into his house on Herengracht. The cold atmosphere dampens her spirit until she is given a dollhouse that proves to be an exact replica of her new home. This historical novel by Jessie Burton brings the Golden Age back to life.

**Ober** – If you want to understand Dutch humour, then you have to watch the films by Alex van Warmerdam. *Ober* is a black comedy all about Edgar, who works as a waiter in a drab restaurant in Amsterdam. When his downtrodden life gets the better of him, he turns to the author writing the story of his life and asks him to change the script.

**A Noble Intention** – Based on a true story, this film adaption of the classic Dutch novel by Thomas Rozenboom is set in late 19th century Amsterdam. The construction of the main station has just been completed and the luxurious Victoria Hotel is supposed to be built across the street. But a stubborn violin maker refuses to let his little old house be torn down. And, in fact, the house still stands on the same spot today.

**Dutch Light** – Wonderful, award-winning documentary by Pieter-Rim de Kroons (2003) about the special quality of light on Dutch Old Master paintings. It shows many works from the Rijksmuseum, landscapes in and around Amsterdam and interviews with museum directors and artists

When the ex-Queen goes to the movies, then only the Tuschinski will do

## MUZIEKGEBOUW AAN 'T IJ
(132 B3) *(𝄞 H3)*

The concerts in the two halls of this glass palace on the water are usually devoted to contemporary music. The walls, ceiling and floor of the hall are movable so that the acoustics can be perfectly tuned to every kind of music. *Piet Heinkade 1 | www.muziekgebouw.nl | tram 26 Muziekgebouw*

## HET MUZIEKTHEATER ★
(129 D5) *(𝄞 G4)*

When it was opened in 1986 this forbidding-looking modern complex on Waterlooplein was controversial. Over time, the people of Amsterdam have come to accept it because it gave them a new city hall as well as the only opera house in the Netherlands. Their name for the monumental edifice is *Stopera,* fusing Stadhuis (city hall) and opera. In the foyer, INSIDER TIP free lunchtime concerts are held on Tuesdays at 12:30pm from Sept. to May. *Waterlooplein 22 | tel. 020 6 25 54 55 | tram 9, 14 Waterlooplein*

## THEATRE

### BOOM CHICAGO (131 D5) *(𝄞 E3)*
Founded in 1993 by a couple of American comedians, Boom Chicago has become a real institution in Amsterdam. The stand-up and other comedy acts performed in English draw on current events, often with a touch of political satire. In the Rozentheater | Rozengracht 117 | *tel. 020 4 23 01 01 | www.boomchicago. nl | tram 10, 13, 14, 17 Marnixstraat/Rozengracht*

### STADSSCHOUWBURG ★
(135 F1) *(𝄞 E5)*

In 1894, the municipal theatre opened on Leidseplein with an ornate Neorenaissance façade. Its stage is the scene for major productions of classic drama in Dutch such as works by Ibsen and Chekhov. In summer, it plays host to many international performances of the Holland Festival. *Leidseplein 26 | tel. 020 6 24 23 11 | tram 1, 2, 5, 7, 10 Leidseplein*

# WHERE TO STAY

**Although there are approximately 460 hotels with 67,000 beds in Amsterdam, it's not easy to find a good room at a reasonable price. The city boasts 14 million overnight stays per year. Prices are high, standards are not; a double room, even in a basic hotel is hard to find for less than 120 euros.**

If style and atmosphere matter to you, then you'll have to pay more – and often book incredibly early. On no account should you arrive without a room reservation! In the peak season (Easter to October) hotels, B & Bs, and AirBnB rooms in all price categories are often booked out months in advance. There are a few real gems amongst Amsterdam's hotels. They include big, luxury hotels with a long tradition and B&Bs hidden away in crooked buildings on canals. The latter are often quite charming but sometimes come with the odd drawback such as alarmingly steep stairs or draughty windows. One thing to watch out for is that many small hotels don't take credit cards! Value added tax is included in the price, but a tourist tax of 5% is usually added on top. If you arrive by car, don't forget to ask about parking when you book. Parking on the street is very expensive in the city centre. Hotels without their own parking spaces sometimes have permits for guests or special deals with local car parks. You can book a hotel room online at *www.hotels.nl* or directly with *Iamsterdam, www.iamsterdam.com*. If you fancy a night on the water, search *www.houseboathotel.nl*

## Modern on the waterfront, gently rocking on a canal or traditional style in the centre: in Amsterdam rooms are not cheap but they have charm

or INSIDER TIP accomodation on houseboats. You can also search *AirBnB (www.
airbnb.com)* under the keyword "boot"
to turn up a number of offers for rooms
on houseboats.

### HOTELS: EXPENSIVE

### AMERICAN HOTEL
135 F1) *(M E5)*

A wonderful Art Nouveau building. Although the rooms have been modernised,
some of the old-fashioned leaded glass

windows remain. Don't miss the Grand
Café on the ground floor. *188 rooms |
Leidsekade 97 | tel. 020 5 56 30 00 |
www.edenamsterdamamericanhotel.
com | tram 1, 2, 5, 7, 10 Leidseplein*

### ANDAZ ⭐
(131 D6) *(M F4)*

The star Amsterdam designer Marcel
Wanders has turned the former library
on Prinsengracht into a luxury design
hotel. Neo-baroque opulence mixes
with a good dose of humour inside. The

85

A noble residence on the canal:
The Dylan

rooms are decorated in an original style with free-standing washbasins.
*122 rooms | Prinsengracht 587 | Tel. 020 5 23 12 34 | www.amsterdam.prinsengracht.andaz.hyatt.com| Tram 7, 10 Raamplein*

### COLLEGE HOTEL
(135 F3) *(ØJ F7)*
The Amsterdam school of hotel management operates this luxurious boutique hotel in an attractive 19th-century school building near Museumplein. Spacious rooms, friendly staff. *40 rooms | Roelof*

*Hartstraat 1 | tel. 020 5 71 15 11 | www thecollegehotel.com | tram 3, 5, 12, 24 Roelof Hartplein*

### THE DYLAN ★ (131 D5) *(ØJ F4)*
An upmarket design hotel in a 17th-century canal house. The owner, designer Anouska Hempel, has gone to town with opulent striped fabrics and dark colours – she knows no taboos, not even walls painted black. Guests have a choice between seven different room styles, from classic and antique to Asian and minimalist. *41 rooms | Keizersgracht 384 | tel 020 5 30 20 10 | www.dylanamsterdam. com | tram 13, 14, 17 Raadhuisstraat*

### ESTHERÉA (128 A4) *(ØJ F4)*
This third-generation family-run business is situated in a total of six converted canal houses. Although the hotel was recently renovated, the 1930s style has fortunately been kept. *70 rooms Singel 303–309 | tel. 020 6 24 51 46 www.estherea.nl | tram 13, 14, 17 Raadhuisstraat*

### GRAND HOTEL AMRÂTH AMSTERDAM
(132 A4) *(ØJ H3)*
The imposing early 20th-century Scheepvaartgebouw has been home to the Amrâth Hotel for a few years now. The foyer and staircase were restored according to the original design and the Art Deco style of the building guided the furnishing of the spacious high-ceilinged rooms. *165 rooms | Prins Hendrikkade 108 | tel. 020 5 52 00 00 www.amrathamsterdam.nl | 10 min. walk from the main station*

### NH GRAND HOTEL KRASNAPOLSKY
(128 B3) *(ØJ F3)*
This is indisputably the "grande dame" of Amsterdam's hotels. Breakfast and lunch are served in the heart of this imposing

Neoclassical building on the Dam, which is the INSIDERTIP conservatory with its great glass dome that is a protected historical architectural feature. Gustav Mahler ate breakfast here at one time. *469 rooms | Dam 9 | tel. 020 5 54 91 11 | www. nh-hotels.com | tram 13, 14, 16, 24, Dam*

## MÖVENPICK AMSTERDAM
(132 B4) (*ØØ H3*)

The Mövenpick Hotel with its 408 stylish and modern rooms occupies a striking high-rise on the IJ. If you book a room ☆ as high up as possible on the west side, you will have a terrific view across the water and the city! *Piet Heinkade 11 | tel. 020 5 19 12 00 | www.moevenpick-hotels.com | tram 26 Muziekgebouw*

## W AMSTERDAM (128 A3) (*ØØ F3*)

Chic design hotel with a young clientele located directly behind Dam. A trendy bar is located on the uppermost floor, complete with a rooftop terrace and an outdoor pool where you can splash above the rooftops of Amsterdam. *238 rooms | Spuistraat 175 | tel. 020 8 11 25 00 | www.wamsterdam.com | tram 1, 2, 5, 13, 14, 17 Dam*

## HOTELS: MODERATE

### ARENA ★ (137 D2) (*ØØ J5*)

This hotel with minimalist styling in a former orphanage caters primarily to a young clientele. Some of the rooms are split over two floors. *116 rooms | s'Gravesandestraat 51 | tel. 020 8 50 24 00 | www.hotelarena.nl | tram 6, 7, 10 s'Gravesandestraat*

### CANAL HOUSE ★ (131 E4) (*ØØ F3*)

Its American owner has combined two 17th-century canalside houses to create this stylish accommodation. All rooms

have lovely old wooden floors, none have a TV. The breakfast room looks onto an overgrown garden. *23 rooms | Keizersgracht 148 | tel. 020 6 22 51 82 | www.canalhouse.nl | tram 13, 14, 17 Westermarkt*

## CONSCIOUS HOTEL VONDELPARK ☺
(134 C2) (*ØØ C6*)

One of Amsterdam's first true eco-hotels located at the southern end of Vondelpark. It consumes 20 per cent less energy than comparable accommodation, uses only biodegradable cleaning materials, and puts fair-trade products on the breakfast table. *81 rooms | Overtoom 519 | tel. 020 8 20 33 33 | www.conscious shotels.com | tram 1 Overtoomsesluis*

---

**MARCO POLO HIGHLIGHTS**

★ **Andaz**
Neo-baroque temple on Prinsengracht → p. 85

★ **The Dylan**
Sumptuously decorated design hotel → p. 86

★ **Arena**
Minimalist design and trendy guests in a former orphanage → p. 87

★ **Canal House**
A hotel with lots of atmosphere, thanks to antiques and a wild garden → p. 87

★ **Amstel Botel**
Inexpensive hotel anchored in the NDSM shipyard → p. 90

★ **Citizen M**
Self-service design hotel at a budget price → p. 90

**DE FILOSOOF** (135 D2) (*⌂ D5*)
Hotel in a quiet street near Vondelpark. Every room is dedicated to a philosopher or writer. The Aristotle room is Greek-inspired, the walls of the Goethe room are adorned with quotes from Faust. *28 rooms | Anna van den Vondelstraat 6 | tel. 020 6 83 30 13 | www.hotelfilosoof.nl | tram 1, 6 Overtoom*

**HOTEL V FREDERIKSPLEIN**
(136 B2) (*⌂ G6*)
Design hotel conveniently located between Utrechtsestraat and Albert Cuyp-markt. Relatively small rooms, but they are equipped with flatscreen TVs and comfortable beds. The lobby is more like a lounge bar – and it even has a fireplace. *48 rooms | Weteringschans 136 | tel. 020 6 62 32 33 | www.hotelv.nl | tram 7, 10 Frederiksplein*

**THE HOXTON**
(128 A4) (*⌂ F4*)
Offshoot of a small English design hotel chain. Super location in 5 merchant houses on Herengracht. Locals also frequent the bar. *111 rooms | Heren-*

# MORE THAN A GOOD NIGHT'S SLEEP

### Industrial Revitalization
A total of three five-star suites can be found at the *Faralda Kranhotel (O) (⌂ O) (NDSM-Plein 78 | tel. 020 760 61 61 | www.faralda.com | free ferry from the main station to the NDSM ship-yard)* situated in the former port crane of the NDSM shipyard. Two panoramic lifts take you to the whirlpool, where you can relax at a height of 50 metres (164 ft.). VIPs and international DJs treasure the experience and are willing to pay 500 euros per night for it.

### Tailored to Taste
*The Exchange* **(128 B3)** (*⌂ G3*) *(from 100 euros | Damrak 50 | tel. 020 5 23 00 80 | www.hoteltheexchange. com | tram 4, 9, 16, 24 Dam)* is just the right place for fashionistas. All of the hotel's 61 rooms have been "clothed" in an original way by graduates of the Amsterdam Fashion Institute. If you feel inspired by your surroundings, you can also give it a go, because each room has a sewing machine.

### Hotel? No thanks!
Are hotel rooms too boring for you? How about spending the night in a streetcar, behind a secret door hidden in a bookcase or in a house within a house? The affordable rooms in *Hotel Not Hotel* **(130 B6)** (*⌂ C4*) *(23 rooms | Piri Reisplein 34 | tel. 020 8 20 45 38 | www.hotelnothotel.com | tram 7, 17 Witte de Withstraat)* are spread out throughout a large communal living space, rounded off by the cocktail bar *Kevin Bacon*.

### Miniature Realm
A boiler house from 1897 that used to belong to the Waterworks now houses Amsterdam's smallest hotel – *De Wind-ketel* **(130 C2)** (*⌂ D2*) *(from 325 euros for two nights | Watertorenplein 8c | info@windketel.nl | www.windketel.nl | tram 10 Westerpark)*. The single two-person suite is furnished with pieces by Dutch designers and stretches over three floors.

racht 255 | tel. 020 88 85 55 | www.the
oxton.com | tram 13, 17 Dam

Is design your thing? The colourful
lobby of the Lloyd Hotel

### INSIDER TIP LLOYD HOTEL
33 D4) (*K3*)

rt and design hotel in a magnificent
uilding on the eastern harbour islands
nat was once a hostel for people emi-
rating with the Lloyd shipping line. 116
ndividually furnished rooms. *Oostelijke*
*andelskade 34 | tel. 020 5 613636 |*
*ww.lloydhotel.com | tram 10 C. van Ee-*
*terenlaan*

### IR. JORDAN (131 D4) (*E3*)

1r. Jordaan is uncomplicated and
ezellig" – just like the Jordaan dis-
rict itself. Located in its namesake
istrict, the lovely old canal house has
4 rooms. *Bloemgracht 102 | tel. 020*
*25 5801 | www.mrjordaan.nl | tram 10*
*loemgracht*

### INSIDER TIP PENSION HOMELAND
32 B4) (*J3*)

ntil 2016, the naval base was a hidden
o-go area in the middle of the city. Then
ie Royal Navy left, and the former offic-
rs' quarters were turned into the Pen-
ion Homeland. This accommodation
bounds in retro charm because every-
iing has been kept in true 1970s style.
ie restaurant offers delicious meals and
>vely seating on the harbour basin of
osterdok. Sometimes swimmers jump
ght into the water from the patio. *31*
rooms | Kattenburgerstraat 5 | tel. 020
23 25 50 | www.pensionhomeland.com |
us 48 Kattenburgerstraat

### HO
28 B3) (*G4*)

iis affordable and pleasant little hotel
ts on a quiet side street off the Dam.
ie building was once a theatre, and the
:age has been turned into a common

space and breakfast room. *105 rooms |*
*Nes 5–23 | tel. 020 6 2073 71 | www.rho*
*hotel.com | tram 4, 9, 16, 24 Dam*

### SEVEN BRIDGES (136 B1) (*G5*)
You really can see seven canal bridges
from this hotel. Each room is individually
furnished, all of them with antiques and
art. Ask for the INSIDER TIP room with a
fireplace! *11 rooms | Reguliersgracht 31 |*

*tel. 020 6 23 13 29 | www.sevenbridges hotel.nl | tram 4, 7, 10 Frederiksplein*

### SIR ADAM (132 A2) *(𝄞 G2)*

The bottom eight floors of the A'DAM tower were transformed into this "urban luxury boutique" hote. Raw concrete walls and vintage furniture set the tone. *108 rooms | Overhoeksplein 7 | tel. 020 2 15 95 10 | www.siradamhotel.com | free*

# LOW BUDGET

*Cocomama* **(136 B2)** *(𝄞 G2) (from approx. 30 euros for a bed in a shared 6-bed room; approx. 50 euros for a double room | Westeinde 18 | tel. 020 6 27 24 54 | www.cocomama.nl | Tram 4, 7, 10 Frederiksplein)* is a "Boutique-Hostel" that combines authentic, beautifully decorated rooms with the sociability of a hostel – including the antics of the resident tomcat Joop.

The *Volkshotel* **(137 D3)** *(𝄞 H6) (rooms from 69 euros | Wibaut-straat 150 | tel. 020 2 61 21 00 | www.volkshotel.nl | metro Wibautstraat)* is a budget hotel with a good measure of design in a building full of creative studios. The club-restaurant is located on the 7th floor, and the sauna is on the roof.

The *CityHub* **(130 B6)** *(𝄞 D4) (from 50 euros | Bellamystraat 3 | www.cityhub.com | tram 3, 7, 12, 17 Bilderdijkstraat/Kinkerstraat)* is not for claustrophobics. The communal areas are spacious, but the rooms, or rather room pods, are stacked on top of each other with low bunks.

*ferry from the main railway station t Buiksloterweg*

### TOREN (131 E4) *(𝄞 F3)*

Hotel by the Westerkerk, run by the sam family for generations. The 40 rooms ar divided between two 17th-century cana houses. Nice garden. *Keizersgracht 164 tel. 020 6 22 60 33 | www.toren.nl | tram 13, 14, 17 Westermarkt*

### HOTEL SPA ZUIVER ● (0) *(𝄞 0)*

This spa hotel on the edge of the Am sterdamse Bos woods is just right if you want peace and natural surrounding The room price includes use of the poo sauna and gym. The metro takes you t the centre of Amsterdam in 15 minute *31 rooms | Koenenkade 8 | tel. 020 3 0 07 10 | www.spazuiver.nl | metro 51 A. Ernststraat*

### AMSTEL BOTEL ★ (129 E2) *(𝄞 0)*

The crossing on the free ferry from the main station to a former shipyard i the Noord district takes only 15 min utes. The botel, which tends to attrac party-goers, is docked here, crowned b the 5 "Loftletters": a hotel room with special design theme is situated in eac of the letters in "BOTEL". *175 rooms NDSM-Pier 3 | tel. 020 6 26 42 47 | www amstelbotel.nl*

### CITIZEN M ★ (135 E5) *(𝄞 E8)*

Seldom has the concept of a budget de sign hotel be carried out as thoroughl as at Citizen M. The tiny but very stylish rooms have king-size beds, LCD te evisions and tropical-rain showers. Th ground-floor lounges also have designe furnishings. There is no reception and self-service bar instead of a restauran *215 rooms | Prinses Irenestraat 30 | te*

You can see seven bridges from the hotel Seven Bridges

020 8 11 70 90 | www.citizenm.com | tram 5 Prinses Irenestraat | metro 50, 51 Zuid WTC

## DWARS (136 B–C2) (ω G5)

Nine small but charmingly decorated rooms can be found in a side street off Utrechtsestraat. No breakfast, but there are many cafés located around the corner. Utrechtsedwarsstraat 79 | Tel. 06 19 55 56 51 | www.hoteldwars.com | tram 4 Prinsengracht

## EUPHEMIA (136 B2) (ω F5)

Hotel in a former monastery near Leidseplein. Relaxed atmosphere, plain and good-value rooms. 15 rooms | Fokke Simonszstraat 1–9 | tel. 020 6 22 90 45 | www.euphemiahotel.com | tram 16, 24 Weteringscircuit

## DE HALLEN (130 C6) (ω D4)

Since the former tram depot is a listed building, the 55 rooms were built in as a free-standing unit. The lovingly furnished foyer features art and lounge seating. The Foodhallen next door offer plenty of options for a bite to eat (see p. 58). 55 rooms | Bellamyplein 47 | tel. 020 8 20 86 70 | www.hoteldehallen.com | tram 3, 12 Kinkerstraat

## LINDEN (131 D3) (ω E2)

Casual hotel in the Jordaan district with small rooms but a good breakfast. 20 rooms | Lindengracht 25 | tel. 020 6 22 14 60 | www.lindenhotel.nl | tram 3 Marnixplein

## MUSEUMZICHT (135 F2) (ω F5)

The name tells you what you get: a view of the Rijksmuseum opposite. The owner used to be an antiques dealer, which is why every corner of the breakfast room is crammed full. Take care on the extremely steep stairs! 14 rooms | Jan Luykenstraat 22 | tel. 020 6 71 29 54 | tram 2, 5 Hobbemastraat

## ST CHRISTOPHER'S INN
(128 C3) (ω G3)

This hotel in the red light district also houses a bar and the discotheque Winston Kingdom. Most of the 67 rooms were styled by artists and designers, and even the ground-floor toilet is a miniature gallery. *Warmoesstraat 123–129 | tel. 020 6 23 13 80 | www.st-christophers.co.uk/amsterdam-hostels | 10 min. walk from the main station*

**THE TIMES** (128 A2) *(F3)*
3-star accommodation on the loveliest stretch of the Herengracht. If you want to enjoy the view, make sure to book a "Grachten Room"! *34 rooms | Herengracht 137 | tel. 020 3 30 60 30 | www.thetimeshotel.nl | tram 1, 2, 5, 13, 17 Nieuwezijds Kolk*

## PRIVATE ACCOMMODATION

**B28** (128 B1) *(F3)*
A historic sailing ship has found a new role as a B&B on Herengracht, providing accommodation for two in the heart of Amsterdam. *Herengracht 28g | tel. 06 29 03 59 56 | www.b28.nl | 5 min. walk from the main station* | *Budget*

**BED & BREAKFAST BOVEN IJ**
(132 C1) *(K1)*
This pretty double room in an old dyke house in Amsterdam-Noord comes with free parking. The bus and ferry take you to the city centre in just 10 minutes. *Leeuwarderweg 50 | tel. 020 4 21 89 56 | www.bbbovenij.nl | bus 32, 33, 38 Merelstraat* | *Budget*

**THE FLYING PANCAKE** (136 C1) *(H5)*
Upmarket bed & breakfast with two suites in an 18th-century house where designer washbasins meet antique furniture. *Nieuwe Kerkstraat 15 | tel. 06 38 30 52 19 | www.theflyingpancake.com | metro Waterlooplein* | *Moderate*

**INSIDER TIP LEVANT B & B**
(133 E4) *(L3)*
It would be hard to find more typical accommodation than this old barge in the eastern harbour district. The larg cabin is fitted out for two guests and has its own bathroom. *Levantkade 90 www.levantbb.nl | tram 10 Azartplein* *Moderate*

**MIAUW SUITES** (131 E5) *(F3)*
Two bright, 70-square-metre (754 sq. ft. apartments with living room, bedroom and kitchen facilities. Conveniently lo cated for shopping on the 9 *straatjes Hartenstraat 3 | tel. 020 717 34 29 | www miauw.com | tram 13, 14, 17 Weste markt* | *Expensive*

**MS LUCTOR** (131 E2) *(F1)*
B & B with three attractive cabins in an old barge in the Westerdok harbour basin near the main station. The ship is powered by solar energy, and guests can explore the city by bicycle or canoe without leav ing a carbon footprint. *Westerdok 103 | te 06 22 68 95 06 | www.boatbedandbreak fast.nl | bus 48 Barentszplein* | *Moderate*

**B & B SILODAM** (131 E1) *(F1)*
65-square-metre (700 sq. ft.) apart ment in an old silo building with a view of the timber harbour. *Silodam 129 | te 06 34 30 30 38 | www.bb-silodam.nl | bus 48 Barentszplein* | *Budget*

**STUDIO INN** (131 E1) *(F1)*
Two well-lit double rooms offer a view of the Westerdok. The larger room has a fridge and a dining table on which lo cal organic products are served for breakfast. If you are travelling in a group of four, you can also book the smaller room next door. *Barentszplein 3 | tel. 06 14 77 68 65 | www.studio-inn.nl | bus 48 Barentszplein* | *Budget*

**SUITE 2 STAY** (136 B2) *(G5)*
Two holiday apartments in a quiet street at the edge of the historic quarter. The

If you don't want to pitch your tent at Camping Zeeburg, book one of the colourful caravans

round-floor studio has a simple, modern style, but the one on the first floor as neo-Baroque furnishings. Both uites can accommodate two to three eople. *Fokke Simonszstraat 76a | tel. 6 10 01 46 41 | www.amsterdamsuitestay. om | tram 4, 7, 10, 16, 24 Weteringcir-uit | Budget*

## HOSTELS

**LINKNOORD** (132 A2) (*Ø H2*)
ip, young hostel in an old laboratory uilding that belonged to Shell Oil. The uge lobby is an exhibition space, a ar, and a kitchen for guests all rolled to one. *213 rooms | Badhuiskade 3 | el. 020 71 83 94 00 | www.clinkhostels. om | free ferry from the main station to uiksloterweg*

**TAYOKAY VONDELPARK** (135 E2) (*Ø E5*)
Vhat makes this hostel so attractive is s top location in a large villa situated irectly on Vondelpark. Beds approx. 19

euros. *500 beds | Zandpad 5 | tel. 020 5 89 89 99 | www.stayokay.com | tram 1, 2, 5, 7, 10 Leidseplein*

## CAMPING

**CAMPING VLIEGENBOS** (133 D1) (*Ø K1*)
This camp site is hidden in a little forest. It also offers platform tents and cabins situated around a shared kitchen. From 10.50 euros per person, 7 euros per car. *April–Oct | Meeuwenlaan 138 | tel. 020 6 36 88 55 | www.vliegenbos.com | bus 32, 33, 38, Merelstraat*

**CAMPING ZEEBURG** (0) (*Ø 0*)
This year-round campsite lies on an island in the IJmeer to the east of Amsterdam. You can rent a **INSIDER TIP** colourful little caravan or a cabin. The nearest tram stop is about 10 min. walk away. From 7 euros per person, 5 euros per car. *Zuider IJdijk 20 | tel. 020 6 94 44 30 | www.campingzeeburg.nl | tram 26 Zuiderzeeweg*

# DISCOVERY TOURS

## 1 AMSTERDAM AT A GLANCE

**START:** ❶ Westermarkt
**END:** ❶ Westermarkt

**Distance:**
🚶 9 km/5.6 miles

1 day
Walking time
(without stops)
2 hours

**COSTS:** tram ticket 2.80 euros per ride
❸ Westertoren: entrance fee 7.50 euros
❺ Het Grachtenhuis: entrance fee 12 euros
❼ Rijksmuseum: entrance fee 15 euros

If there is one thing that is absolutely characteristic of Amsterdam, then it is the un constrained mix of historic architecture and modern urban life. On this full day tou experience the glory of the past in the city of canals and let yourself be carried awa by the hustle and bustle of this modern-day shopper's paradise.

Would you like to explore the places that are unique to this city? Then the Discovery Tours are just the thing for you – they include terrific tips for stops worth making, breathtaking places to visit, selected restaurants and fun activities. It's even easier with the Touring App: download the tour with map and route to your smartphone using the QR Code on pages 2/3 or from the website address in the footer below – and you'll never get lost again even when you're offline.

**TOURING APP**

→ p. 2/3

0:00am The ideal day in Amsterdam begins no earli-
r than 10am with a small breakfast, perhaps near the
Westermarkt. **Leave the market square and head
orth for a bit on the west side of the Keizersgracht. Turn
ft down the Leliegracht and cross the bridge at the end
get to the west side of the Prinsengracht. Continue
eading north past the next bridge, then look to your
ft where you will find** the very typical ❷ INSIDER TIP
afé t'Smalle *(Egelantiersgracht 12).* Its small but sunny

**❶ Westermarkt**

**❷ Café t'Smalle**

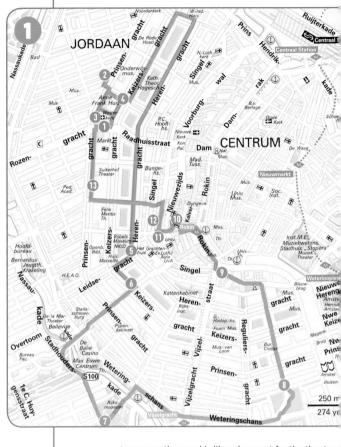

terrace on the canal is like a box seat for the theatre summer. The next destination can already be seen fro here: the unmistakable **③ Westertoren** → p. 43, whic towers **above the other side of the Prinsengracht**. If yo climb up this church tower – the highest in Amsterda – you will be rewarded with a wonderful view of the a most entirely preserved historic city centre with all i many facets.

**11:00am** Once you are back on the ground, it is now tim to take a closer look at the **④ Grachtenring (Canal Rin** → p. 37 on foot. **Turn right just behind the Westerke and then take the next left to reach the Keizersgrach**

**③ Westertoren**

**④ Canal Ring**

he canal is lined by a row of elegant 17th-century state-
houses, and thanks to the legendary *lack of curtains*
p. 25, you can take a peek at some of the marbled in-
eriors with their moulded ceilings. **Stroll along the ca-
al towards the north.** Most of the canal houses have
imple brick façades, but every now and then you will
ome across something different, such as the **house with
eads** *(Keizersgracht 123)*, on the right-hand side of the
treet whose façade is graced with the busts of Greek
ods. **Continue northwards until you reach the Brouw-
rsgracht,** which is ringed by former warehouses of the
cal breweries, and **then turn right. Cross over the small
ut pretty pedestrian bridge to get to the Herengracht**,
which is the most stylish of the three main canals. **Walk
n for about ten minutes towards the south** until you
ome across ❺ **Het Grachtenhuis** → p. 41, where you can
arn about the history of the canal ring.

**01:00pm** By now it's time for lunch and your stomach
s probably rumbling. **Walk south just a bit further and
urn right at the next corner onto the snug Leidsegracht
nd then head left on the Keizersgracht** to get to the
ovely café-restaurant ❻ **Morlang** → p. 58 where you
an relax on the terrace right on the water. After a bite
o eat, hop aboard **tram no. 2 or 5 at the stop on Keiz-
rsgracht and head off to the** ❼ **Rijksmuseum** → p. 49.
Once you leave the modern foyer, the ornate interior of
his impressive building will transport you back in time.
or a few hours you can delve into the world of the Gold-
n Age in the wonderfully beautiful historic galleries
nd admire famous masterpieces by Rembrandt and his
ontemporaries as well as a small, but fine collection of
sian art.

**04:00pm** If you need a breath of fresh air after taking in
he paintings, grab a bench in the **Museum's Gardens**
nd watch the kids playing gleefully in the fountains. Af-
erwards, **go through the pedestrian tunnel to the north
nd cross the Museumbrug to Weteringsschans. From
he tram stop Spiegelgracht, take tram no. 7 or 10 to
rederiksplein.** You'll need to keep an eye on your wal-
et here, but not because of pickpockets: opposite the
ark to your left, ❽ **Utrechtsestraat** → p. 68 stretches
o the north, lined by all kinds of enticing little shops and
afés. Taste some home-made chocolate in the **Choco-
aterie Van Soest** *(No. 143)* and shop for some designer

❺ Het Grachtenhuis

❻ Morlang

TRAM 2, 5 KEIZERSGRACHT
❼ Rijksmuseum

TRAM 7, 10 FREDERIKSPLEIN
❽ Utrechtsestraat

⑨ Tuschinski

⑩ Begijnhof

⑪ Café Hoppe

⑫ D'Vijff Vlieghen

⑬ Vyne

❶ Westermarkt

clothes at **Look Out** *(No. 91)* or gifts at **Jan → p. 73** *(No. 74)*. At **the end of Utrechtsestraat, you will find the chaotic Rembrandtplein. From the northwest corner of the square, head down Reguliersbreestraat, which will take you to Muntplein.** Take a look at the foyer of the cinema ⑨ **Tuschinski → p. 82** with its splendidly sinister Art-Déco decor. **From Muntplein, turn diagonally to the right onto Rokin, and then turn left onto the Spui. Behind the inconspicuous wooden door within the white façade on the right-hand side of the square,** the ⑩ **Begijnhof → p. 30** awaits. This somewhat hidden oasis in the midst of all the shoppers on the streets is not too overrun with tourists shortly before it closes at 5pm.

**06:00pm** Afterwards, join the Amsterdammers for *borreluur* (akin to happy hour) and drink a strong beer from the local *Brouwerij 't IJ* in the historic Stehpub ⑪ **Café Hoppe → p. 36** located on the **western side of the Spui**. If you want to end the day in old Dutch style, go **a few metres further north on Spuistraat** to the restaurant ⑫ **D'Vijff Vlieghen → p. 62**. After your meal, **head north along the street and then turn left onto Raamsteeg. Cross over Singel, Herengracht and Keizersgracht, and then turn right down the Prinsengracht.** Order a glass of wine and enjoy the view of the canal in the popular bar ⑬ **Vyne → p. 78** before returning to the start of the day's tour, the ❶ **Westermarkt** around 10pm.

# AMSTERDAM FOR FOODIES

| START: ❶ Centraal Station | 1/2 day |
| END: ❶ Centraal Station | Walking time (without stops) |
| Distance: | 1 hour |
|  4 km/2.5 miles | |

**IMPORTANT TIPS:** Bring a big appetite on this tour because it crosses through the Wallen, stopping at one fine food shop after the other. It is best to plan this tour for an afternoon (because of the opening times of the sampling venues).

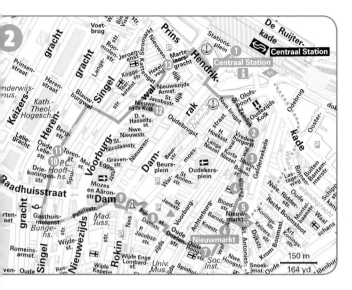

Amsterdam is not exactly known as a paradise for food connoisseurs. Yet the city of canals has been shaped by its long history as a trading hub for culinary wares such as grain, coffee, tea and spices. On this walk, you will discover that this metropolis of the Netherlands definitely has something to offer any gourmet. Come with us to the heart of the medieval city centre and explore the world of Amsterdam's culinary specialities.

**03:00pm** From the very beginning, food has played an important role in Amsterdam as it has always been a city of trade. About 700 years ago, when the city's first residents built a dam to connect the banks of the Amstel, a bustling market soon appeared where fishermen from near and far sold their wares. Goods from around the world were shipped over the river or the sea to Amsterdam and sold directly from the harbour. This market was located exactly where the ❶ **Centraal Station → p. 32**, Amsterdam's main station, stands today – and **it also marks the beginning of this walking tour. From the square in front of the station, head south and turn left before the Hotel Victoria to get to the tip of Zeedijk**. To get off to a good start, enjoy a good cup of coffee in the quaint ❷ **Hofje van Wijs** *(Zeedijk 43)*. This coffee and tea shop was founded in 1792 and is the official purveyor to the court. The Dutch love their coffee and the annual per cap-

ita consumption of their quite strong brew tops ou at 150 litres.

Pepped up by your coffee buzz, **take a walk down Zeedijk**. You will soon notice Chinese street signs and shops as you have now arrived in Amsterdam's **Chinatown → p. 33**. On the corner of Stormsteeg, pop in one of the oldest Asian shops in the city, ❸ **Toko Dun Yong**. This family-owned shop first opened its doors in 1959. Asian food is stacked on the shelves on the ground floor while woks, steam baskets and other items can be found on the three upper stories. In the evening, *cooking workshops (cooking.dunyong.com)* are held on the first floor.

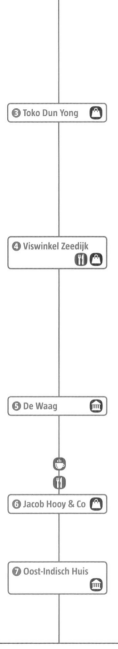

❸ Toko Dun Yong

❹ Viswinkel Zeedijk

❺ De Waag

❻ Jacob Hooy & Co

❼ Oost-Indisch Huis

**04:00pm** Pass by the displays of peking duck and colourful rice cakes and **continue along Zeedijk.** Just when you feel like you are really in Hong Kong or Shanghai, you will stumble across the tiny shop at No. 129 ❹ **Viswinkel Zeedijk**, which sells aromatic smoked fish and particularly good Dutch brined herring (*maatjes*). The herring trade was an important economic sector in Amsterdam from the very beginning and street names such as *Haringpakkerssteeg* or *Zoutsteeg* (salt path) still attest to this. Even if you are not a fan of this fatty fish, you should give the herring here a try. According to true connoisseurs, the pickles and onions usually served with *maatjes* actually mask the true taste of the fish and should be left out.

A market has been held every day for centuries on the **Nieuwmarkt → p. 35**. The stalls cluster around ❺ **De Waag → p. 36**, which was once part of the city gate and served as the official weigh house from 1618 onwards. Merchants had their wares weighed on the calibrated scales to make sure that they were not being cheated when they bought grain or wheels of cheese. Today, the former weigh house is surrounded by cafés and pubs as well as small delis, ice cream shops, Asian fast food counters and ❻ **Jacob Hooy & Co → p. 70**, an herbalist's shop with a long tradition. Relatively early on, all kinds of herbs, seasonings and exotic spices were available in Amsterdam thanks to the presence of the Dutch East India Company. The company's former headquarters was **located around the corner in ❼ Oost-Indisch Huis,** which you can get to by **walking along Kloveniersburgwal and then turning right onto Oude Hoogstraat.** Take a look at the lovely courtyard of this building designed by the architect Hendrick de Keyzer!

`05:00pm` **Continue walking down the busy streets Oude Hoogstraat and Damstraat until you reach Oudezijds Voorburgwal. Take a right and then a quick left and you will find yourself in the narrow Pijlsteeg,** where the tiny emporium of ⑧ **Wynand Fockink → p. 79** is hidden at the end of the road. Give the *Superior Gerijpte Genever* a try. Your glass will be poured to the brim so you will probably have to bend down and slurp the first few sips. With a little lift in your steps, **continue on to** ⑨ **Dam → p. 26,** a square which was home to the fish market in the 16th century – freshwater fish were sold on the east side and saltwater fish on the west. To the left, you will find the filled-in harbour of Rokin. A bit further along, the shopping street Kalverstraat runs into the square where calves were once driven to the livestock market.

**Leave the** Koninklijk Paleis **→ p. 32 to the right behind you and follow Paleisstraat to the former city moat called Singel, where you should turn right. Across from Toren-sluis bridge,** at Singel 184, a true temptation awaits: the designer pralines from ⑩ **Puccini → p. 71** whose ingredients confirm that the Dutch still love to experiment with spices and flavours. If you are more in the mood for something savoury, then head a few doors

⑧ Wynand Fockink 🍷

⑨ Dam 🏛

⑩ Puccini 🛍🍴

An herbal paradise: At Jacob Hooy & Co, it feels like it is still the heyday of the Dutch East India Company

**⑪ Reypenaer**

**⑫ In de Wildeman**

**⑬ Automatiek FEBO**

**❶ Centraal Station**

down to **⑪ Reypenaer** *(Singel 182)*. The cheese shop sell fine cheeses naturally ripened in an old warehouse nea Utrecht and offers regular tastings *(Mon/Tue 1pm, 3pm, Wed–Sun noon, 1:30pm, 3pm, 4:30pm)*. When you've had your fill, **continue along the canal to the north and then turn right at the first bridge onto the narrow Li jnbaanssteeg,** which is home to the long-standing butch er's shop **Reinhart**. Their *ossenworst* – a raw beef sausage seasoned with nutmeg and cloves – is famous throughou the Netherlands. The best place to try it is in the pub **⑫ In de Wildeman → p. 78**, accompanied by a local beer, per haps from *Brouwerij 't IJ*. To get to the pub, **head along Nieuwezijds Voorburgwal a bit to the north and then turn right onto Nieuwezijds Kolk. The pub is hidden a few me tres behind a small picturesque house, built in 1620, tha belonged to the Kornmessergilde (corn appraisers' guild)**

06:00pm **From here, follow along Nieuwezijds Voor burgwal to get back to the start of the day's tour.** Ha your appetite been whet by all the sampling you've don and are you ready for something more substantial? Then head to the **corner of Nieuwendijk** where you will find th famous, or rather infamous, **⑬ Automatiek FEBO** *(Nieu wendijk 50)*. Select something like a warm meat croquette from the vending machine and munch away as you strol back to **❶ Centraal Station**.

---

# 3 EXPLORE REJUVENATED NEIGHBOURHOODS

| START: **❶ Lijnbaansgracht/Rozensgracht** END: **⑫ De Gouden Reael** | 1/2 day Walking time (without stops) 1.25 hours |
|---|---|
| Distance: **⇒ 4.5 km/2.8 miles** | |

**IMPORTANT TIPS:** tram no. 10, 13, 14, 17 to the starting point at Marnixstraat/Rozengracht

★ **Jordaan** used to be the home of Amsterdam's poor. With its small and simple houses, this neighbourhood is a contrast to the elegance of the canal ring. The seething smells of the old workshops on the western harbour islands are now a thing of the past. Both these districts have become popular residential areas with their own particular charm. This walking tour will take you through the other side of Amsterdam's Golden Age without all the wealth and grandeur.

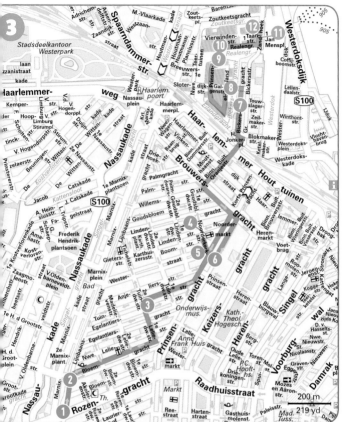

**03:00pm** Begin your walking tour at **①** **Lijnbaansgracht at the corner of Rozensgracht and follow along the Lijnbaansgracht to the north for a while.** In earlier days, ropes and cables were strung along this very long canal, which used to lie directly behind the city walls, so that they could be woven. Even Rembrandt came to appreciate the particular charm of this craftsmen's quarter where he set up his atelier in a warehouse on **②** **Bloemgracht** in 1637. To find Rembrandt's canal, **turn right at the second corner.** In the Jordaan district, everything is a bit smaller and cosier than along the canal ring. Quaint houses snuggle next to each other while little bridges span across the tree covered canals. When you walk past the houses at 87 to 91, you will

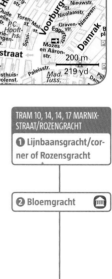

TRAM 10, 14, 14, 17 MARNIX-STRAAT/ROZENGRACHT

**①** Lijnbaansgracht/corner of Rozensgracht

**②** Bloemgracht

find three well-preserved, identical stepped gable houses from the 17th century. **At the end of the canal, turn left down 1e Leliedwarsstraat,** which is home to modern houses as well as ones dating back to the Golden Age. In the 19th century, the Jordaan neighbourhood became home to much of Amsterdam's poor. Many of the old buildings fell into ruin and had to be replaced by newly constructed houses in the 1980s. Nowadays, this quarter is once again a popular place to live, which has something to do with the many nice cafés, galleries and shops that line its streets. If you like to browse around small shops with a distinctive character, then this is the right place for you. For example, **head across the Egelantiersgracht and keep walking straight on until you stumble upon** the nostalgic ❸ **Oud-Hollandsch Snoepwinkeltje** *(2e Egelantiersdwarsstraat 2)* with its shelves full of old-style Dutch sweets and candy.

❸ Oud-Hollandsch Snoepwinkeltje 🛍️

❹ Noorderkerk 🏠

❺ Winkel 43 ☕

❻ Van Brienenhofje 🏛️

A row of pretty canal houses: De Gouden Reael is on the far right

**04:00pm** **Continue along Tuinstraat and then head left down Prinsengracht until you reach** ❹ **Noorderkerk** → p. 42, the main Protestant church in Jordaan. If you are already a bit hungry, then try a piece of Dutch apple cake *(Appeltaart)* on **Noordermarkt** → p. 73 in the café ❺ **Winkel 43** or, if it happens to be Saturday, buy a snack at the organic farmer's market. **Afterwards, keep going north, cross the bridge Lekkeresluis and take a look at the houses at numbers 85 to 133 on the other side of the Prinsengracht.** Here you will find the picturesque ❻ **Van Brienenhofje** *(Mon-Fri 6am–6pm, Sat 6am–2pm)*. These *Hofjes* were houses funded by merchants as residences for low-income elderly people living on their own. Today, there are still 46 of these hidden oases with their lovingly tended court-yards located in Jordaan.

**05:00pm** **Walk back across the same bridge and head towards the northwest along Brouwersgracht. Cross over the Oranjebrug to the right. A few minutes later, you will pass under the train tracks to get to Hendrik Jonkerplein.** The western harbour is ands – Bickerseiland, Prinseneiland and Realeneiland – an all be seen from here. Originally, all the factories or usinesses that made too much noise or stink for the up-tanding city centre were banned to these islands. Tar and alt works, roperies, shipyards and fish processing plants ettled on the water's edge. Warehouses were built behind hem and soon thereafter houses were put up for workers nd seamen. Today, almost all of the former workshops ave been turned into sought-after flats and artists' atel-ers. Cross over the square to ⑦ **Bickersgracht**. Old brick ouses, cobblestones and overgrown canal gardens lend his street a nostalgic charm. It is quite hard to believe that his area was considered one of the city's worst places to ve in the 1960s. **On the other side of the canal,** you can ross the small bridge to get to ⑧ **Prinseneiland**. **Galgen-traat** is the name of the lane behind the bridge because he gallows that were located on the northern banks of he River IJ could be seen from here. The pretty warehous-s that line the entire island belie the rather morbid history f this street. Their names such as De Windhond, De Teer-on or De Witte Pelicaan are prettily illustrated on the ga-les or painted ornately on the shutters. **Follow the street n Prinseneiland clockwise and walk around the south ide of the island.**

**06:00pm** On the north end of the island, cross over the ⑨ **Drieharingenbrug** to get to ⑩ **Realeneiland**. This pic-uresque drawbridge was named after the house "De rie Haringen" located on the other side of the canal. The **Realengracht**, whose banks are lined with small ship-ards, is home to many bobbing houseboats made from ld cargo barges. Right around the corner, you will find he quay called ⑪ INSIDER TIP▶ **Zandhoek,** whose name omes from the sand market that was established on his spot in 1634. A row of impressive canal houses long this pier are a symbol of the wealth of some of the merchants who once lived here. Inside the last house, ⑫ **De Gouden Reael**, you will find a lovely café-restau-ant with a sunny terrace on the waterfront. It is the per-ect place to enjoy a glass of wine or a meal at the end f the day's walk around 6pm. When you are ready to ead home, **cross the bridge behind the Gouden Re-ael and walk down the street to Westerdoksdijk. Just round the corner to the right, you will find the bus top for No. 48 (to Borneo Eiland), which runs to the main station.**

⑦ Bickersgracht

⑧ Prinseneiland

⑨ Drieharingenbrug

⑩ Realeneiland

⑪ Zandhoek

⑫ De Gouden Reael

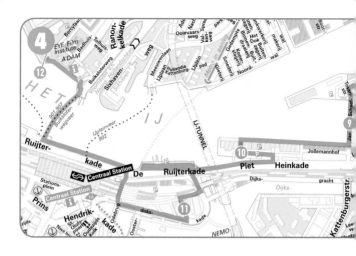

## 4

# MODERN ARCHITECTURE ON THE WATER

🚲 **START:** ① Lloyd Hotel
**END:** ⑫ Eye Film Institute

🏛🏢🛍
🌞☕🍸

**Distance:**
➡ 10.5 km/2.8 miles

**1/2 day**
Cycling time
(without stops)
45 minutes

**COSTS:** bicycle rental approx. 12 euros

In recent years, interesting architectural structures have been built in Amsterdam especially along the banks of the IJ. The harbour landscape has been transformed from the industrial look of the past into a modern urban space. The islands Java, KNSM and Borneo-Sporenburg have been turned into young residential areas that are quite sought-after with their experimental architecture. The area around the main station has also been revitalised by the construction of new cultural buildings.

| ① Lloyd Hotel 🏛 | **09:00am** The best way to explore the new architecture along the water is in typical Dutch style with a bike *(rentals → p. 117)*. **Swing onto the saddle and peddle on to the** ① **Lloyd Hotel → p. 89**. Originally built as a home for emigrants by the Lloyd shipping company in 1918, it was reopened as a design hotel in 2005. Take a look at the surprisingly light-filled restaurant to get an impression of this transformation. **From the IJ harbour on the opposite side** you can get a first look at the INSIDER TIP islands and their |
| --- | --- |

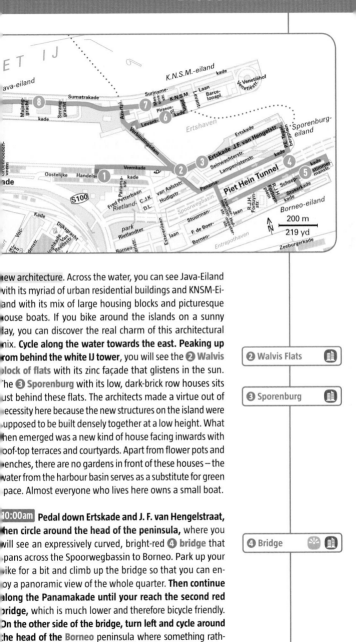

new architecture. Across the water, you can see Java-Eiland with its myriad of urban residential buildings and KNSM-Eiland with its mix of large housing blocks and picturesque house boats. If you bike around the islands on a sunny day, you can discover the real charm of this architectural mix. **Cycle along the water towards the east. Peaking up from behind the white IJ tower,** you will see the **② Walvis block of flats** with its zinc façade that glistens in the sun. The **③ Sporenburg** with its low, dark-brick row houses sits just behind these flats. The architects made a virtue out of necessity here because the new structures on the island were supposed to be built densely together at a low height. What then emerged was a new kind of house facing inwards with roof-top terraces and courtyards. Apart from flower pots and benches, there are no gardens in front of these houses – the water from the harbour basin serves as a substitute for green space. Almost everyone who lives here owns a small boat.

**10:00am** Pedal down Ertskade and J. F. van Hengelstraat, then circle around the head of the peninsula, where you will see an expressively curved, bright-red **④ bridge** that spans across the Spoorwegbassin to Borneo. Park up your bike for a bit and climb up the bridge so that you can enjoy a panoramic view of the whole quarter. **Then continue along the Panamakade until your reach the second red bridge,** which is much lower and therefore bicycle friendly. **On the other side of the bridge, turn left and cycle around the head of the Borneo** peninsula where something rath-

**②** Walvis Flats

**③** Sporenburg

**④** Bridge

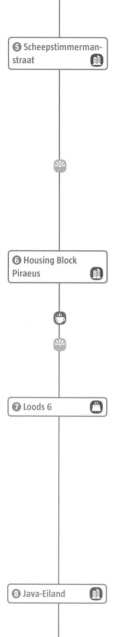

**⑤ Scheepstimmerman-straat** 📖

**⑥ Housing Block Piraeus** 🏢

**⑦ Loods 6** 🛍️

**⑧ Java-Eiland** 📖

er special awaits. For the first time since the 17th century, the city sold lots to private individuals; the sale of these parcels on ⑤ **INSIDER TIP Scheepstimmermanstraat** was a real exception to the rule in the Netherlands. Buyers were allowed to build a villa in the row designed by their respective architect of choice. A great variety of styles thus emerged. Biking along this street is like passing through a colourful gallery of architectural experiments. Particularly unusual examples include the house at No. 120 with a tree growing through the middle and the house at No. 62, which is clad entirely in wood. For the prettiest view of these houses, **look at them from the small pedestrian bridge to Stokerkade.**

**From here, head along Stokerkade, past a large brown block of flats back to the bicycle bridge and then down Walvis until you get to the dam that leads across to KNSM,** the island of the Koninklijke Nederlands Stoomboot Maatschaaij, the Royal Dutch Steamboat Shipping Company. It is dominated by the large, sculpture-like ⑥ **Piraeus housing block** designed by German architects Kollhoff and Rapp, which encircles the small old building to your right. If you are in the mood to take a little break, the café **Kanis en Meiland** in the Pireaus complex is a nice place to stop. From the waterfront terrace, you can watch the comings and goings on the decks of the houseboats docked in the harbour basin. If you are

in the mood for some designer shopping, the shops on the harbour in ⑦ **Loods 6** directly on the **KNSM-Laan to the north** are just the right thing. At **Sissy Boy** → p. 73 *(No. 19)*, you will find fashion and accessories, while **Pols Potten** *(No. 39)* offers designer home décor items and **Imps & Elfs** *(No. 297)* sells children's clothes and furnishings.

**12:00pm To the west of the dam, KNSM borders** ⑧ **Java-Eiland**. The atmosphere on this island is more urban. Tall hous-

ng blocks line the busy street of Sumatra-Kai on the north ide of the island. **Rather than following the cars, take the parallel route through the lovely and peaceful green zone of the island's interior until you cross left over the ⑨ Jan-Schaeffer-Bridge.** It ends at the Oostelijke Handelskade beneath the old Wilhelmina packing house that has been transformed into a cultural centre. **Turn right from here and pedal along the fish-shaped cruise ship terminal to the ⑩ Muziekgebouw aan 't IJ → p. 83.** The striking glass concert hall was built by the Danish architects 3XN.

**Wheel along the water away from the bridge, turn right at the first traffic light and cross over De Ruijterkade to get back to Oosterdokseiland.** Take a look around the imposing ⑪ Openbare Bibliotheek → p. 32, the public library with its modern designer furnishings. **Then continue along Oosterdokskade, heading right at the end of the peninsula beneath the train tracks and then left along the water. After a few hundred metres, you will reach the ferry terminal behind the main station. Hop aboard the free ferry that heads to Buiksloterweg to get to the north shore,** where the futuristic ⑫ Eye Film Institute → p. 53 marks the end of the tour around 1pm. Give your legs a little rest and enjoy an aperitif on the waterfront terrace or in the spectacular foyer space of this one-of-a-kind arena.

⑨ Jan-Schaeffer-Bridge

⑩ Muziekgebouw aan 't IJ

⑪ Openbare Bibliotheek

⑫ Eye Film Institute

Contemporary architecture brings personality to the harbour islands

# TRAVEL WITH KIDS

### ARTIS ●
(132 B6) (*M* H4)

Amsterdam's zoo is not particularly large, but it is old and the landscaping is lovely. It is home to 1,400 species from all over the world. One of the aquariums is a real curiosity. It shows a INSIDER TIP microcosm of an Amsterdam canal, including dumped bikes and a wrecked car. *Nov–Feb 9am–5pm, Mar–Oct 9am–6pm | admission 20 .50 euros, children aged 9 & under 17 euros | Plantage Kerklaan 38–40 | www.artis.nl | tram 9, 14 Plantage Kerklaan*

### CANAL BIKE
The best way to explore the canals of Amsterdam is on a canal bike. Rain ponchos are provided if the weather is bad. The pedal-powered boats are moored by the Rijksmuseum *(Stadhouderskade 42)*, on *Leidseplein*, at the Anne Frank Huis *(Prinsengracht 42)*, and at *the corner of Keizersgracht and Leidestraat. 8 euros per person for 1 hour, 11 euros per person for 1.5 hours | www.canal.nl*

### CHILDREN'S FARMS
Every sizeable park in Amsterdam has a free children's farmyard where all kinds of animals – from pigs and cows to guinea pigs – can be admired and sometime petted. For example, *Overbrakerpad 16* (130 B1) (*M* D1) | *Tue–Sun 10am–5pm tram 10 Van Hallstraat*

### INSIDER TIP MICROPIA
(132 B6) (*M* H4)

Yuck might be the first word that come to mind when a microbe museum i mentioned. But, once you take a clos look at these tiny living things, you wil be surprised at their beauty. Molds, m croalgae, bacteria and viruses are the stars of the exhibits in this intriguing museum. Especially children aged 8 an up can boost really boost their micr scopic knowledge. *Sun–Wed 9am–6pm Thu–Sat 9am–8pm | admission 14 euro children aged 9 & under 12 euros | Plan tage Kerklaan 38–40 | www.micropia.nl tram 9, 14 Artis*

### GOAT FARMYARD
(0) (*M* 0)

In the middle of Amsterdam's woodland there is a farmyard full of goats. 150 goats and kids (the four-legged variety roam here, and children can comb an milk them. On Saturdays there are dem onstrations of how cheese is made from fresh goat's milk. *Wed–Mon 10am–5pm*

Floating Dutchmen, XXL bubbles and the secrets of the deep sea: Amsterdam is full of fun surprises waiting to be discovered!

ree admission | Nieuwe Meerlaan 4 | bus *4 Schiphol Oost*

## NEMO

*129 F2–3) (ΩΩ H3)*

his science museum is full of activi-es for kids. They can blow bubbles big nough to stand in, make their own quorice or find out why you can see rough water. Hands-on is the motto ere. In summer there is a ● café with addling pool on the roof. *Daily May–ct, Nov–April Tue–Sun 10am–5:30pm | dmission 15 euros, free for children 3 & nder (MK) | Oosterdok 2 | www.e-nemo. l | 10 min. walk from the main station*

## PANNENKOEKENBOOT

*)) (ΩΩ 0)*

ancakes galore are offered on the *Pan-enkoekenboot*. While the kids decorate eir pancakes with colourful sprinkles, um and dad can enjoy the peaceful our-long round trip across the IJ, from e former timber harbour *(Houthaven)*

to the main station and the eastern harbour islands. *Wed, Fri, Sat, Sun 4pm and 5:45pm, Sat/Sun also at 12:30pm and 2:15pm | adults 17.50 euros, children 3–12 years old 12.50 euros | departure from NDSM-wharf (20 min. ferry ride from the main station) | www.pannenkoekenboot. com*

## TUNFUN

*(129 E5) (ΩΩ H4)*

Originally the plan was to build a car tunnel under the Meester Visserplein. But, the project was abandoned when it was only half finished. It is now the site of the largest indoor playground in Amsterdam. Everything here is a bit bigger than usual from the toy construction site with three cranes to the maze and to the slides and trampolines. Snacks, drinks and even ear plugs can be purchased inside. *Daily 10am–6pm | free admission for adults, children 12 & under 8.50 euros | Meester Visserplein 7 | tram 9, 14 Meester Visserplein*

# FESTIVALS & EVENTS

There is always something going on in Amsterdam, where festivals and events take place year round. More formal concerts are often held outdoors with the canals as a backdrop whilst louder events take over old shipyards or factories. Public holidays are surprisingly few and far between – with just 8 days per year, the Netherlands are at the lower end of the scale in Europe.

## EVENTS

### APRIL

27 April is ● ★ **Koningsdag.** Every year until 2013 the Dutch honoured their Queen on 30 April. With the coronation of Willem-Alexander, this public holiday was moved to his birthday on 27 April. On this occasion, the whole of Amsterdam turns into one great flea market, and hordes of Dutch beer drinkers in orange t-shirts crowd the streets. A big open-air concert is held on Museumplein. If the 27th falls on a Sunday, the celebrations take place on Saturday the 26th.

### MAY

**Bevrijdingsfestival**: The liberation from German occupation in the Second World War is commemorated on 5 May with a all-day open-air festival on Museumple

### JUNE

**Open Tuinen Dagen:** On the third wee end in June, 30 canal gardens open the doors to visitors.

**Holland Festival:** A two-week event which dance and theatre groups fro all around the world make guest a pearances in Amsterdam. The ma venue is the Stadsschouwburg theat on Leidseplein.

INSIDER TIP *The open-air season begi* in Vondelpark. Free music and theat performances until the end of August.

### JULY

**Roots Festival:** A colourful mixture of ternational world music bands perform at different places around the city for te days. The festival concludes with a fre open-air concert in Oosterpark.

**Amsterdam Pride:** spectacular gay p rade on the last weekend in July or th first weekend in August.

### AUGUST

**Grachtenfestival:** The cultural highlig of the Amsterdam summer. The eve

## In Amsterdam there's always a reason to celebrate. Preferably in summer and in a park, on a square or along a canal

at really draws the crowds is the ee ★ *Prinsengrachtconcert* in front of e Pulitzer Hotel in mid-August.

*Pluk de Nacht:* Ten-day open-air film stival at the Stenen Hoofd on the bank f the IJ.

### EPTEMBER

*rdaan Festival:* What started out as neighbourhood party has developed to a large-scale fair with music and ancing.

*pen Monumentendag:* On the second aturday of the month almost all historic onuments in the city are open.

### CTOBER

*rachtenrace:* canal rowing regatta on e second Saturday of the month.

*msterdam Dance Event:* 2,000 inter- ational DJs who spin techno, electro, ouse and hip-hop music visit the city ach year for a 4-day convention. DJ sets nd concerts are offered in the evenings.

### NOVEMBER

On the third Sunday in November *Sinterklaas* (St Nicholas) arrives at the maritime museum by boat and then mounts a horse to ride on to the Dam.

### DECEMBER

5 December is *Pakjesavond* (package eve). Traditionally, the Dutch exchange presents on this day and not on Christmas. Most museums close at 3pm and the streets are empty.

## NATIONAL HOLIDAYS

| 1 Jan | *Nieuwjaar* New Year's Day |
| March/April | Good Friday; Easter Monday |
| 27 April | *Koningsdag* |
| 5 May | *Bevrijdingsdag* (only public institutions are closed) |
| May/June | Ascension Day; Whitmonday |
| 25/26 Dec | Christmas |

# LINKS, BLOGS, APPS & MORE

LINKS & BLOGS

**www.spottedbylocals.com/amsterdam** People who live in Amsterdam reveal their personal tips, from shops to restaurants and clubs. Lots of recommendations off the beaten track

**www.simplyamsterdam.nl** Sightseeing tips, news from Amsterdam and an up-to-date calendar of events

**www.bookatable.com/nl/amsterdam/restaurants** Many popular restaurant in Amsterdam are booked out weeks in advance. On this website you can check whether tables are available and reserve one online immediately

**amsterdamcyclechic.com** Blog about biking around Amsterdam in style

**www.amsterdamfoodie.nl/blog/** Restaurant reviews and other culinary musings written by a British woman living in Amsterdam

**www.tripadvisor.co.uk/ShowForum-g188553-i58-The_Netherlands.html** This well-known online forum gives you the opportunity to put all your questions about Amsterdam

**www.facebook.com/iamsterdam** Facebook community of the city marketing organisation "I amsterdam". Visitors to Amsterdam can put their questions about what's on in the city and post photos, links that they like and other recommendations

**www.facebook.com/AmsterdamCanals** Facebook page filled with beautiful as well as strange photos featuring Amsterdam's canals

**www.amsterdamoldtown.com** All about Amsterdam's Old Town, from Chinatown to the Red Light district. With tips from locals and descriptions of the places of interest as well as of activities in this colourful quarter

Regardless of whether you are still preparing your trip or already in Amsterdam, these addresses will provide you with more information, videos and networks to make your holiday even more enjoyable.

www.amsterdamacoustics.com Films by international musicians who perform acoustic versions of their tracks on the streets in Amsterdam. Many of them are alternative bands, but a few better-known artists are among them

www.youtube.com/watch?v=sTPsFIsxM3w Facts to counter prejudices: this likeable film defends the city of Amsterdam against claims that it is a hotbed of anarchists

www.geobeats.com/videoclips/netherlands/amsterdam/jordaan An entertaining introduction to the Jordaan quarter – courtyards, churches and the Anne Frank House

www.youtube.com/watch?v=a09_wVSBkyw Amsterdam 100 years ago: not surprisingly, the biggest difference between this old footage and the urban scene today is the lack of cars on the streets

vimeo.com/104016366 This animated film tells the story of the city's growth from the Middle Ages until the completion of the canal ring

GVB App This app by the city transportation company GVB tells you how to find the nearest tram stop wherever you may be, and when the next one will come along

Spotted by Locals App Amsterdam If you have an iPhone, you can install the *Amsterdam Local Tips* to get ideas for seeing the sights and where to eat, leaving the tourist hordes behind

UAR App For architecture fans this *Layar App UAR* has been produced by the *Arcam* centre for architecture to provide information on the spot about buildings in Amsterdam – and it even includes those that are yet to be buil

City Cards App Whoever buys an *I amsterdam City Card* can also download the corresponding app. It offers detailed information about the city's sights and special offers that are part of the City Card programme as well as a digital map of the city

Rijksmuseum App The Rijksmuseum offers a well-designed app for Android and iPhone devices that replaces the classic audio tour. It features several guided tours as well as information about individual artworks

# TRAVEL TIPS

## ARRIVAL

🚆 Centraal Station has direct connections from major cities in western Europe, including high-speed Thalys links from Paris, Brussels and Cologne. From Britain, there are connections at Brussels with trains from London through the Channel Tunnel operated by Eurostar (tel: 08705 104 105; www.eurostar.com), with good-value through-fares to Amsterdam.

✈ Amsterdam Schiphol Airport has excellent connections to other European cities as well as intercontinental flights to North America. From Schiphol, about 11 miles southwest of the city, trains run every 15 minutes to the main station (journey time 20 min., fare 4 euros). A taxi to the city centre costs 45 euros. If you are staying in a 4- or 5-star hotel, the KLM shuttle bus will take you there, departing twice hourly. Schiphol: tel. 0900 0141 | www.schiphol.nl.

🚗 If you are driving, Amsterdam is easy to reach on the excellent Dutch motorway network, but congestion around and especially in the city mean this is not the recommended way to arrive. If you do drive, consider using the park and ride system, leaving your car at one of a number of points on the ring motorway A10: at Sloterdijk station, Zeeburgereiland, the Olympic stadium, Bos en Lommerplein and the Amsterdam Arena. On weekdays prior to 10am, you can park for 8 euros for the first 24 hours and then euro per each additional 24 hours. If you park after 10am or at the weekend, the first 24 hours only cost 1 euro. The price of the tickets for public transportation into the city range from 5 euros for 1 person to 7.70 euros for 5 people. For more information, check out www.iamsterdam.com

## RESPONSIBLE TRAVEL

It doesn't take a lot to be environmentally friendly whilst travelling. Don't just think about your carbon footprint whilst flying to and from your holiday destination but also about how you can protect nature and culture abroad. As a tourist it is especially important to respect nature, look out for local products, cycle instead of driving, save water and much more. If you would like to find out more about eco-tourism please visit: www.ecotourism.org

## BICYCLE HIRE

Don't get into the saddle in Amsterdam unless you are used to cycling and feel confident because the traffic is chaotic. But if you're up for it, a INSIDER TIP bike trip through the city is a memorable experience. Costs for bike hire start at 10 euros for 24 hours.
– ● Star Bikes (De Ruyterkade 127 | tel. 020 6 20 32 15 | www.starbikesrental. com)
– Rent A Bike (Damstraat 20–22 | tel. 020 6 25 50 29 | www.bikes.nl)
– Mac Bike (Weteringschans 2, Leidseplein | De Ruijterkade 34b, main station | Oosterdokskade 149 | Waterlooplein 199 | tel. 020 6 20 09 85 | www.macbike.nl)

## CANAL TOURS

…Vhat would a trip to Amsterdam be with-…ut a canal tour? A number of companies …un these tours, most of them starting …rom the main station or in front of the …ijksmuseum. In terms of programme …nd prices there is little difference. Tick-…ts can be purchased online, but usually …ou won't have to wait long if you just …urn up, as the daytime tours start every …0 minutes. A one-hour trip takes you …hrough the Canal Ring and Golden Arc, …he Jordaan quarter, out onto the IJ, into …he Oosterdok harbour basin and usually …long a stretch of the Amstel. Recorded …xplanations are given in English and …ther languages. The price is about 15 …uros with, for example, *Rederij Lov-…rs (tel. 020 5 30 10 90 | www.lovers.nl); …msterdam Canal Cruises (tel. 020 6 79 …3 70 | www.amsterdamcanalcruises.nl); …oathouse (tel. 020 3 37 97 33 | www. …eeamsterdam.nl).* Evening cruises with …r without a meal are also offered (see p. …0). Environmentally friendly canal trips …n ⓥ gas-powered boats are operated …y *Canal Hopper (128 C2) (⌀ G3) (Dam-…ak 6 | www.canal.nl | tel. 020 2 17 05 00).* ´ou can also hire a boat powered by green …lectricity from ● ⓥ **INSIDER TIP** *Boaty …136 B4) (⌀ F7) (from 79 euros for 3 hours, …nax. 6 people | Jozef Israëlskade | walk 50 …m (54 yd.) from Ferdinand Bolstraat along …he Amstel canal | tel. 06 27 14 94 93 | …ww.boaty.nl | tram 12 Scheldestraat).*

## CONSULATES & EMBASSIES

**BRITISH CONSULATE IN AMSTERDAM** *Koningslaan 44 | tel. 020 6 76 43 43 | www.ukinnl.fco.gov.uk*

# CURRENCY CONVERTER

| £ | € | € | £ |
|---|---|---|---|
| 1 | 1.09 | 1 | 0.92 |
| 3 | 3.28 | 3 | 2.75 |
| 5 | 5.46 | 5 | 4.58 |
| 13 | 14.20 | 13 | 11.90 |
| 40 | 43.70 | 40 | 36.63 |
| 75 | 82 | 75 | 68 |
| 120 | 130 | 120 | 110 |
| 250 | 273 | 250 | 229 |
| 500 | 546 | 500 | 458 |

| $ | € | € | $ |
|---|---|---|---|
| 1 | 0.84 | 1 | 1.19 |
| 3 | 1.69 | 3 | 3.56 |
| 5 | 4.22 | 5 | 5.93 |
| 13 | 11 | 13 | 15.42 |
| 40 | 34 | 40 | 47.44 |
| 75 | 63 | 75 | 89 |
| 120 | 101 | 120 | 142 |
| 250 | 211 | 250 | 296 |
| 500 | 422 | 500 | 593 |

For current exchange rates see www.xe.com

**CONSULATE OF THE USA IN AMSTERDAM**
*Museumplein 19 | tel. 020 5 75 53 30 | amsterdam.usconsulate.gov*

## CUSTOMS

Unlimited goods for personal use can be imported and exported without paying duties within the European Union. If you come from outside the EU, other restrictions apply, such as 200 cigarettes, 4 litres of wine, 16 litres of beer, and 1 litre of spirits (22% or more).

## EMERGENCY

Ambulance, police, fire brigade: *tel. 112*; emergency doctor: *tel. 088 0 03 06 00*

## EVENTS

You can find a list of cultural events on the website *www.iamsterdam.nl*. It is best to buy tickets directly from the event website; same-day last minute tickets with a 50 per cent discount are sold at *www.lastminuteticketshop.nl*. The English-language *A-Mag* listing all kinds of events is published every other month. It can be purchased from VVV branches and many news agents for 3.50 euros, but many hotels and restaurants offer free copies.

## GUIDED TOURS

Amsterdam is a good place to explore on foot. English-language tours through the historic districts are operated by big travel agencies and by companies such as *Local Experts (tel. 020 4 08 51 00 | www.local-experts.com)* and *TopTour (tel. 020 6 20 93 38 | www.toptours.net)*. Both companies also offer themed walking tours, such as through the red light district and the INSIDER TIP *hofjes* in Jordaan. The price per person ranges between 15 and 25 euros, depending on the tour.

Almost every bike-hire agency offers guided bike tours. The most comprehensive tour programme, including trips out to the IJsselmeer, can be found at *Orange*

# WEATHER IN AMSTERDAM

| | Jan | Feb | March | April | May | June | July | Aug | Sept | Oct | Nov | Dec |
|---|---|---|---|---|---|---|---|---|---|---|---|---|
| Daytime temperatures in °C/°F | 5/41 | 5/41 | 9/49 | 13/55.5 | 17/62.5 | 20/68 | 22/71.5 | 22/71.5 | 19/66 | 14/57 | 9/49 | 6/43 |
| Nighttime temperatures in °C/°F | 1/34 | 1/34 | 3/37.5 | 6/43 | 9/49 | 12/53.5 | 15/59 | 15/59 | 12/53.5 | 8/46.5 | 5/41 | 2/35.5 |
| ☀ Sunshine hours/day | 2 | 2 | 4 | 6 | 7 | 7 | 6 | 6 | 5 | 3 | 2 | 1 |
| ☂ Precipitation days/month | 14 | 11 | 9 | 9 | 9 | 9 | 11 | 11 | 12 | 12 | 14 | 13 |
| ≈ Water temperature in °C/°F | 5/41 | 5/41 | 6/43 | 8/46.5 | 11/52 | 13/55.5 | 16/61 | 17/62.5 | 16/61 | 14/57 | 10/50 | 8/46.5 |

☀ Sunshine hours/day  ☂ Precipitation days/month  ≈ Water temperature in °C/°F

*ike* (128 C3) (*♫ G3*) (Buiksloterweg 5c | tel. 06 46 84 20 83 | www.orangebike.nl) and *Yellow Bike* (128 B2) (*♫ G3*) (Nieuwezijds Kolk 29 | tel. 020 6 20 69 40 | www. yellowbike.nl | tram 1, 2, 5, 13, 17 Kolk). Prices are around 20 euros for 3 hours including bike hire.

Bus tours of Amsterdam can also be booked, for example the *Hop-on-Hop-off Bus* (128 C2) (*♫ G3*) (Daily 9:15am–5:15pm | 21 euros for 24 hours | Damrak 6 | www.citysightseeingamsterdam. nl | 2 min. walk from the main station), which stops at twelve major sights. Bear in mind, however, that the streets of the old quarter are narrow, which means that buses can only go along the main roads. If you are looking for an eco-friendly way to get around Amsterdam without walking or pedalling yourself, consider taking a tour on a *Segway* electro-scooter (tel. 088 0 12 30 50 | www.seg waybooking.com). With prices starting at 0 euros for 90 minutes including driving instruction, they are by no means cheap, but it's a load of fun to scoot around.

## HEALTH

If you need medical aid, contact a general practitioner (huisarts). The huisarts emergency service is available 24 hours a day: tel. 088 0 03 06 00. In the Netherlands the European Health Insurance Card (EHIC) is accepted. Private travel medical insurance is still advisable, and is essential for visitors from outside the European Union.

## I AMSTERDAM CITY CARD

The *I amsterdam City Card* for leisure and cultural activities is valid for one, two or three days. This chip card gives you a canal trip at a reduced price or even free of charge, use of public transport and free admission to several museums, e.g. the Van Gogh Museum, Amsterdam Museum and Stedelijk museum. It also includes discounts for some other attractions and restaurants. The pass costs 57 euros (1 day), 67 euros (2 days), 77 euros (3 days), or 87 euros (4 days). It is sold at offices of the VVV and online at www.iamsterdam.com.

## INFORMATION IN ADVANCE

### NETHERLANDS BOARD OF TOURISM & CONVENTIONS IN LONDON
*2nd floor Portland House | SW1E 5RS London | www.iamsterdam.com and www. holland.com*

### NETHERLANDS BOARD OF TOURISM IN NEW YORK
*215 Park Avenue South | New York, NY 10003 | tel. (212) 370-7360 | www.holland. com*

## INFORMATION IN AMSTERDAM

### AMSTERDAM TOURIST OFFICE
The tourist offices offer information and tickets for city tours. They will also find you a hotel or B & B for a fee. In the peak season expect to stand in a long queue at the office on Stationsplein!

– *Stationsplein 10 (opposite the main station) | Mon–Sat 9am–5pm, Sun 9am–4pm*

– *Schiphol Airport (arrivals hall) | daily 7am–10pm | tel. 020 7 02 60 00 | www.vvv.nl*

## INTERNET & WIFI

Internet cafés are almost nonexistent in Amsterdam, but various cafés and restaurants offer free internet access. At www. wifi-amsterdam.nl, you will find a city map showing these places. Free WiFi is provided by the *public library (see p. 32)* on

Oosterdokskade and in the area around *de Waag (see p. 36)* on the Nieuwmarkt.

## MONEY & PRICES

The currency in the Netherlands is the euro. At a supermarket checkout don't be surprised if you get only 50 cents change when it should be 52 cents because everything is rounded to 5 cents. 1 and 2 cent coins are rare. Payment by card is common, even for small amounts. In most restaurants, shops and supermarkets you can pay with a debit card (with the Maestro symbol) and PIN code. Many cafés and small restaurants don't accept credit cards. If you want to pay with a credit card, you must know the PIN code.

## OPENING HOURS

On weekdays, most shops are open 9am–6pm, although some small shops do no open until noon or stay closed on Mondays. On Thursdays, city-centre shops stay open until 9pm. On Saturdays you can shop until 6pm, and on Sundays

## BUDGETING

| Coffee | 2.50 euros |
| | *in a koffiehuis for a cup of koffie verkeerd* |
| Beer | 2 euros |
| | *for a glass of beer (0.2 litres)* |
| Cinema | 10 euros |
| | *for a ticket* |
| Tulips | 5 euros |
| | *for 10* |
| Lunch | 10 euros |
| | *for a basic lunch* |
| Tram | 2.90 euros |
| | *for a tram ticket* |

in the city centre from noon until 5pm. Supermarkets open Mon–Sat until 8pm and in the city centre Mon-Sat until 10pm, on Sundays until 8pm. Market stalls close down around 4pm.

## PARKING

There is no free parking within the A10 motorway ring. Parking tickets are bought from machines. You can only pay by debit or credit card, not in cash. Enter your number plate and then choose how many hours or select and all-day or evening ticket. You can get a receipt, but you don't need to put a ticket behind the windscreen. Costs in the city centre *5 euros per hr, day ticket 45 euros (9am–midnight)*. Parking is cheaper outside the centre. The fine for not getting a ticket is 55.50 euros. The much-feared wheel clamps are only used for repeat offenders. The fee if you do get towed away is 373 euros. Car parks in Amsterdam city centre *(approx. 40 euros/day)*: Europarking (Marnixstraat 250); Bijenkorf department store, Muziektheater (Waterlooplein), Nieuwezijds Kolk and Byzantium (Tesselschadestraat 1). Park & ride at different locations along the ring motorway (see p. 116). Further information: *www.parkerenindestad.nl*

## PHONE & MOBILE PHONE

For the green telephone kiosks, which are becoming thin on the ground, you need a phone card, obtainable from a newsagent, post office or the tourist office (VVV). Codes: UK *0044*, USA *00*, Netherlands *0031*, Amsterdam *(0)20*

## POST

Most post offices open Mon–Fri 9am–5pm, Sat 9am–1pm. However, there are wer of them than there used to be. amps are on sale in the *Bruna* chain of ewsagents and at the checkouts in the *bert Heijn* supermarkets. It costs 1.25 eu- s to send a postcard or a standard-sized tter to any place abroad. *www.postnl.nl*

## PUBLIC TRANSPORT

ublic transport in Amsterdam consists trams, buses and a few metro lines. e tickets are chip cards, which cost 90 euros for 1 hour and are valid for e whole of Amsterdam. It is cheaper to y a day ticket or one for several days. ay tickets are valid for 24 hours, cost 50 euros and are sold by the conductor. ckets for several days are sold only at /B Ticket & Info in front of the main sta- on, from machines at metro stops and some hotel receptions. If you arrive at e airport, you can buy an *Amsterdam avel Ticket* that also includes transport and from Schiphol–Amsterdam by ain; it costs 15 euros for 1 day, 20 euros r 2 days or 25 euros for 3 days.

u should usually hop aboard the trams the back door where the conductor ts. The rule for all chip cards is that u have to check in when you board d check out again when you leave the am, even if you are only changing lines! do this, hold the ticket in front of the ader by the conductor's cabin or at the or until the reader beeps. If you forget check out, the ticket loses its validity. nsterdam-Noord is served by buses and ee ferries, which all dock on the north de of the main station. Only the ferry Buiksloterweg runs all night, the oth- s until about midnight. On weekdays uses and trams run until around mid- ght, at weekends until about 1am. After at, there are night buses with special es. A single ticket costs 4.50 euros and valid for 1.5 hours. *www.gvb.nl*

## TAXIS

Cab ranks can be found at places such as the main station (only g eco-taxis will be permitted here starting in 2018), in front of big hotels and on major squares like Leidseplein. It's rather difficult to hail taxis on the street, as many simply don't stop. Even if the drivers tell you some- thing different, you are free to choose which taxi you take! Electric taxis are also available. Basic rate 2.95 euros plus 2.17 euros per km | tel. 020 7777777 | www. tcataxi.nl.

Some companies now specialise in elec- tric taxis, such as Taxi Electric (tel. 088 100 44 44 | www.taxielectric.nl). In the city centre, you can also find bike taxis that you can hail down on the street or book by phone, for example under tel. 06 24 22 77 53. The ranks for bike taxis are located on Rembrandtplein and Leidseplein. A trip for two passengers costs 10 euros for 15 minutes.

## TELEPHONES & MOBILES

Amsterdam's green telephone boxes are becoming quite rare, but if you do find one, you'll need a calling card, which you can purchase from news agents, at the post office, or in VVV branches. Pre- paid SIM cards can be had from 5 euros, and you can purchase top-up vouchers at supermarkets and other stores. Country codes: UK *0044*, USA *001*, Aus- tralia *0061*, Ireland *0353*, Netherlands *0031*, Amsterdam *(0)20*.

## TIPPING

In taxis, restaurants and cafés you round up the amount to be paid to make a tip of five to ten per cent. For room service in a hotel 1–2 euros per day.

# USEFUL PHRASES DUTCH

## PRONUNCIATION

To help you with the pronunciation we have added to each word or phrase a simplified guide on how to say it [in square brackets]. Here kh denotes a guttural sound similar to "ch" in Scottish "loch", and ü is spoken like "u" in French "tu".

### IN BRIEF

| | |
|---|---|
| Yes/No/Maybe | ja [ya]/nee [nay]/misschien [miss-kheen] |
| Please/ | alstublieft [ashtübleeft]/alsjeblieft |
| Thank you | [ash-yer-bleeft]/bedankt [bedankt] |
| Excuse me | Sorry [sorry] |
| May I ...?/ Pardon? | Mag ik...? [makh ick]/ Pardon? [*spoken as in French*] |
| I would like to.../ | Ik wil graag... [ick vill khraakh]/ |
| Have you got...? | Heeft u...? [hayft ü] |
| How much is... | Hoeveel kost...? [hoofayl kost] |
| I (don't) like that | Dat vind ik (niet) leuk. [dat find ick (niet) lurk] |
| broken/doesn't work | kapot [kapott]/werkt niet [vairkt neet] |
| Help!/Attention!/ | Hulp! [hülp]/Let op! [lett opp]/ |
| Caution! | Voorzichtig!/[forzikhtikh] |
| Ambulance | ambulance [ambülantser] |
| Police/Fire brigade | politie [politsee]/brandweer [brandvayr] |

### GREETINGS, FAREWELL

| | |
|---|---|
| Good morning!/afternoon!/ evening!/night! | Goedemorgen/Goedemiddag! [khooyermorkhe/ khooyermidakh]/ |
| | Goedenavond!/Goedenacht! [khooyenafond/khooy- enakht] |
| Hello!/goodbye! | Hallo! [hallo]/Dag! [daakh] |
| See you | Doei! [dooee] |
| My name is... | Ik heet... [ick hayt] |
| What's your name? | Hoe heet u? [hoo hayt ü]/Hoe heet je? [hoo hayt ye] |
| I'm from... | Ik kom uit... [ick komm owt] |

### DATE AND TIME

| | |
|---|---|
| Monday/Tuesday | maandag [maandakh]/dinsdag [dinnsdakh] |
| Wednesday/Thursday | woensdag [voonsdakh]/donderdag [donderdakh] |
| Friday/Saturday | vrijdag [fraydakh]/zaterdag [zatterdakh] |

# Spreek jij nederlands?

**"Do you speak Dutch?"** This guide will help you to say the basic words and phrases in Dutch.

| | |
|---|---|
| Sunday/holiday | zondag [zonndakh]/feestdag [faystdakh] |
| today/tomorrow/ | vandaag [fanndaakh]/morgen (morkher)/ |
| yesterday | gisteren (khisteren) |
| What time is it? | Hoe laat is het? (hoo laat iss hett] |
| It's three o'clock | Het is drie uur [hett iss dree üür] |

## TRAVEL

| | |
|---|---|
| open/closed | open [open]/gesloten [khesloten] |
| entrance | ingang [innkhang]/inrit [inritt] |
| exit | uitgang [owtkhang]/*(car park)* uitrit [owtritt], *(motorway)* afslag [affslakh] |
| departure/ | vertrektijd [fertrekktayt]/vertrek [fertrekk]/ |
| arrival | aankomst [aankommst] |
| toilets women/men | toilet [twalett]/dames [daamers]/heren [hayren] |
| (not) drinking water | (geen) drinkwater [kheen] drinkvaater] |
| Where is...?/Where are...? | Waar is...? [vaar iss]/Waar zijn...? [vaar zayn] |
| left/right/ straight ahead/ | links [links]/rechts [rekhts]/ rechtdoor [rekhtdor]/ |
| back/close/far | terug [terükh]/dichtbij [dikhtbay]/ver [fair] |
| bus/tram | bus [büs]/tram [tram] |
| U-underground / taxi/cab | metro [metro] / taxi [taxi] |
| bus stop/cab stand | station [stasseeonn]/taxistandplaats [taxistandplaats] |
| parking lot/ | parkplaats [parkplaats]/ |
| parking garage | parkeergarage [parkayrkharager] |
| train station/harbour | station [stasseeonn]/haven [haafen] |
| airport | luchthaven [lükhthaafen] |
| timetable/ticket | dienstregeling [dienstraykheling]/kaartje [kaartyer] |
| single/return | enkel [enkel]/retour [retour] |
| train / track/platform | trein [trayn] / spoor [spoor]/perron [peronn] |
| I would like to rent... | Ik wil graag... huren [ick vill khraakh... hüüren] |
| a car/a bicycle/a boat | een auto [enn owto]/fiets [feets]/boot [boat] |
| petrol / gas station | tankstation [tankstasseeonn] |
| petrol/gas / diesel | benzine [benseen]/diesel [diesel] |

## FOOD & DRINK

| | |
|---|---|
| Could you please book a table for tonight for four? | Wilt u alstublieft voor vanavond een tafel voor vier personen voor ons reserveren? [villt ü ashtübleeft for fannaafont en taafel for feer pairzonen for ons reservayren] |
| on the terrace/ | op het terras [opp het terrass]/ |
| by the window | bij het raam [bay het raam] |
| The menu, please | De kaart, alstublieft. [de kaart ashtübleeft] |

| Could I please have...? | Mag ik...? [makh ick] |
| bottle/carafe/glass | fles [fless]/karaf [karaff]/glas [khlass] |
| a knife/a fork/a spoon | mes [mess]/fork [fork]/lepel [laypel] |
| salt/pepper/sugar | zout [zowt]/peper [payper]/suiker [zowker] |
| vinegar/oil | azijn [azayn]/olie [olee] |
| with/without ice/sparkling | met [mett]/zonder ijs [zonder ays]/bubbels [bübbels] |
| May I have the bill, please? | Mag ik afrekenen [makh ick affraykenen] |
| bill/receipt | rekening [raykening]/bonnetje [bonnetyer] |

## SHOPPING

| Where can I find...? | Waar vind ik...? [vaar finnt ick] |
| I'd like.../I'm looking for... | Ik wil... [ick vill]/Ik zoek... [ick zook] |
| pharmacy/chemist | apotheek [apotayk]/drogisterij [drookhisteray] |
| department store | winkelcentrum [vinkelzentrümm] |
| supermarket | supermarkt [züpermarkt] |
| 100 grammes/1 kilo | 1 ons [onz]/1 kilo [kilo] |
| expensive/cheap/price | duur [düür]/goedkoop [khootkoap]/prijs [prayss] |
| more/less | meer [mayr]/minder [minder] |

## ACCOMMODATION

| I have booked a single/ double room | Ik heb een eenpersoonskamer/tweepersoonskamer gereserveerd [ick hepp en aynperzoanskaamer/ tvayperzoanskaamer khereservayrt] |
| Do you have any... left? | Heeft u nog...? [hayft ü nokh] |
| breakfast/half board | ontbijt [ontbayt]/halfpension [hallfpenseeonn] |
| full board (American plan) | volpension [follpenseeonn] |
| at the front/seafront | naar de voorkant/zee [naar de forkannt/zay] |
| shower/sit-down bath | douche [doosh]/badkamer [battkaamer] |
| balcony/terrace | balkon [balkonn]/terras [terrass] |
| key/room card | sleutel [slurtel]/sleutelkaart [slurtelkaart] |

## BANKS, MONEY & CREDIT CARDS

| bank/ATM | bank [bank]/pinautomat [pinn-owtomaat] |
| cash/credit card | kontant [kontant]/pinpas [pinnpass]/ creditcard [kreditkaart] |

## HEALTH

| doctor/dentist/ paediatrician | arts [arts]/tandarts [tandarts]/ kinderarts [kinderarts] |
| hospital/ emergency clinic | ziekenhuis [zeekenhows]/ spoedeisende hulp [spootayzender hülp] |
| fever/pain | koorts [koorts]/pijn [payn] |

# USEFUL PHRASES

| diarrhoea/nausea | diaree [diaray]/misselijkheid [misselick-hayt] |
| inflamed/injured | ontstoken [ontstoaken]/gewond [khevonnt] |
| pain reliever/tablet | pijnstiller [paynstiller]/tablet [tablett] |

## POST, TELECOMMUNICATIONS & MEDIA

| stamp/letter/ postcard | zegel [zaykhel]/brief [breef]/ aanzichtkaart [aanzikhtkaart] |
| I need a landline phone card | Ik wil graag een telefoonkaart voor het vaste net. [ick vill khraakh en telephonekaart for het faster net] |
| I need a prepaid card for my mobile | Ik zoek een prepaid-kaart voor mijn mobieltje. [ick zook en prepaid-kaart for mayn mobeelt-yer] |
| Where can I find internet access? | Waar krijg ik toegang tot internet? [vaar kraykh ick too-khang tot internet] |
| socket/adapter/ charger | stopcontact [stoppkontakt]/adapter [adapter]/ oplader [oplaader] |
| computer/battery/ rechargeable battery | computer [computer]/batterij [batteray]/ accu [akkü] |
| internet connection/wifi | internetverbinding [internetferbinnding]/wifi |
| e-mail/file/ print | mail [mail]/bestand [bestant]/ uitdraaien [owtdraa-yen] |

## LEISURE, SPORTS & BEACH

| beach/bathing beach | strand [strand]/strandbad [strandbart] |
| sunshade/ lounger | zonnescherm [zonner sherm]/ zonnestoel [zonnerstool] |
| low tide/high tide | laagwater [laakhvaater]/hoogwater [hoakhvaater] |

## NUMBERS

| 0 | nul [nüll] | 15 | vijftien [fayfteen] |
| 1 | één [ayn] | 16 | zestien [zesteen] |
| 2 | twee [tvay] | 17 | zeventien [zerventeen] |
| 3 | drie [dree] | 18 | achtien [akhteen] |
| 4 | vier [feer] | 19 | negentien [naykhenteen] |
| 5 | vijf [fayf] | 70 | zeventig [zerventikh] |
| 6 | zes [zess] | 80 | tachtig [takhtikh] |
| 7 | zeven [zerven] | 90 | negentig [naykhentikh] |
| 8 | acht [akht] | 100 | honderd [hondert] |
| 9 | negen [naykhen] | 200 | tweehonderd [tvayhondert] |
| 10 | tien [teen] | 1000 | duizend [dowzent] |
| 11 | elf [elf] | 2000 | tweeduizend [tvaydowzent] |
| 12 | twaalf [tvaalf] | 10000 | tienduizend [teendowzent] |
| 13 | dertien [dairteen] | 1/2 | half [hallf] |
| 14 | viertien [feerteen] | 1/4 | kwart [kvart] |

# STREET ATLAS

■ The green line indicates the Discovery Tour "Amsterdam at a glance"
■ The blue line indicates the other Discovery Tours

**All tours are also marked on the pull-out map**

Photo: Prinsengracht with the Westerkerk

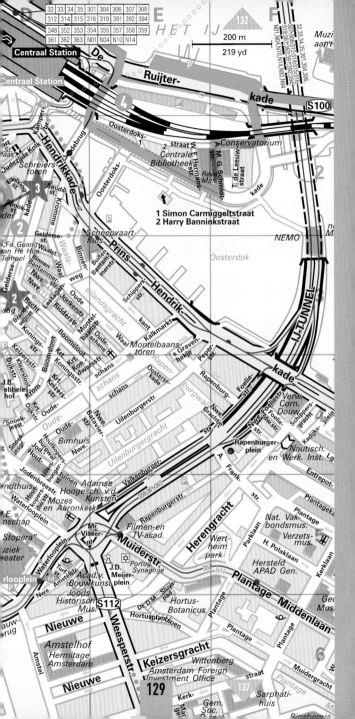

**Centraal Station**

Centraal Station

HET IJ

132

De Ruijter-kade

S100

200 m
219 yd

Muzi
aan't

Oosterdoks-

straat

Centrale
Bibliotheek

W F Hermans-str.

Conservatorium

Revel
Mus.

M. G. Schmidt-
str.

T. de Leeuw-
kade

Schreiers-
toren

St.
aas

Oudezijds Kolk

Smidst-

Kromme

Oosterdoks-

**1 Simon Carmiggeltstraat**
**2 Harry Banninkstraat**

NEMO

ne
M

Hendrikkade

Elleboog-
str.

Nook
der

Recht
Brand
wijnst.

Gelderse-
st.

Waalst.

Fo Guang
an He Hun
Tempel

Gelderse-

Binnen
Bantammer-str.

Nwe.
Bantammer-str.

Scheepvaart-
huis

Prins

Hendrik-

Oosterdok

aag

Konings-
str.

Keizers-
str.

Dijkst.

Boomsloot

Kromme
Waalst.

Binnen
weg

Nwe.
Lastageweg

Oude
Schans

Buiten
Bantam-
merstr.

Schippers-
str.

kant

Kalkmarkt

JJ.TUNNEL

J.B.
ebbeles-
hof

Krt.
Koningsstr.

Krt.
Keizersstr.

Kr. Kon.
dwarsstr.

Montel-
baanstr.

Oude-
schans

Waal

Montelbaans-
toren

's Graven-
hekje

Peper-
str.

kade

/Snoek-
jesst.

Krt.
Krom
Boomssl.

Oude-

Montel-
baanstr.

Oude-
schans

Rapen-
burger-
wal

Rapenburg-

Foelie-
str.

Verw.
Corn.
Douw-

Schippers-
gracht

Snoek-
jesgr.

Oude-
schans

Nwe.
Batavier-
str.

Uilenburgerstr.

Oosterse-
kade

Foelie-
str.

Nwe.

Nwe.
Foelie-
str.

Kadijks-
plein

Bimhuis

Krt.
Houtkopers-
burgwal
Nwe.

Uilenburgergracht

Rapenburger-
plein

Nautisch.
en Werk. Inst.

Entrepot-

Lg

Hout-

Jodenbreestr.
Hoogesch.

Adamse
v.d.
Kunsten

A. Frank-
str.

Plantage

Plantagek.

dthuis

Waterlooplein

Mozes
en Aäronkerk

Rapenburgerstr.

Herengracht

Nat. Vak
bondsmus.

Wert-
heim
park

Parklaan

Plantage

H. Polaklaan

Verzets-
mus.

.E.
nschap

Waterlooplein
plein

Mr.
Visser-
pl.

Filmen-en
TV-acad.

Muiderstr.

Herstelde
APAD Gen.

Kerklaan

Stopera
uziek
eater

Turf-
Amstel-
str.

J.D.
Meijer-
plein

Portug.
Synagoge

Dr. D.M. Sluys-
str.

Geo
Mus

rlooplein

Acad.v.
Bouwkunst

Joods
Historisch
Mus.

Weesperstr.

S112

Hortus-
Botanicus

Plantage Middenlaan

6

uw-
rug

Nieuwe

Amstelhof
Hermitage
Amsterdam

Hortusplantsoen

Plantage

Amstel

Nieuwe

Keizersgracht

Wittenberg
Amsterdam Foreign
Investment Office

129

straat

Muidergracht

Sarphati-
huis

137

Kerk-

Gem.
Soc.

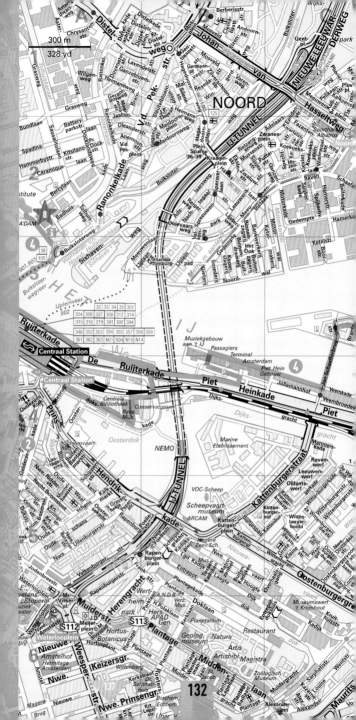

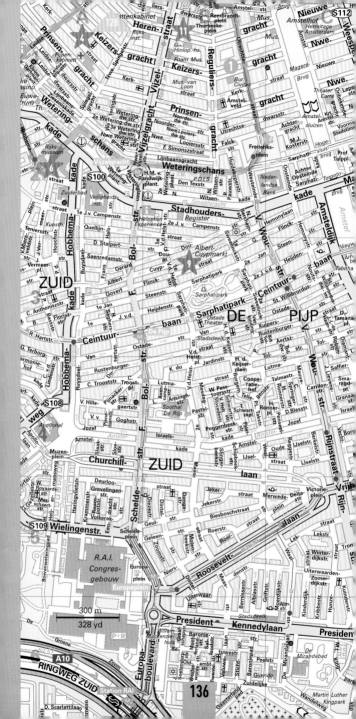

This index contains a selection of the streets and squares shown on the street atla

# KEY TO STREET ATLAS

| | | |
|---|---|---|
| Autosnelweg<br>Autobahn | | Motorway<br>Autoroute |
| Weg met vier rijstroken<br>Vierspurige Straße | | Road with four lanes<br>Route à quatre voies |
| Weg voor dorgaand verkeer<br>Durchgangsverkehr | | Thoroughfare<br>Route de transit |
| Hoofdweg<br>Hauptstraße | | Main road<br>Route principale |
| Overige wegen<br>Sonstige Straßen | | Other roads<br>Autres routes |
| Parkeerplaats - Informatie<br>Parkplatzrk - Information | P    i | Parking place - Information<br>Parking - Information |
| Straat met eenrichtingsverkeer<br>Einbahnstraße | | One way road<br>Rue à sens unique |
| Voetgangerszone<br>Fußgängerzone | | Pedestrian zone<br>Zone piétonne |
| Belangrijke spoorweg met station<br>Hauptbahn mit Bahnhof | | Main railway with station<br>Chemin de fer principal avec gare |
| Overige spoorweg<br>Sonstige Bahn | | Other railway<br>Autres ligne |
| Ondergrondse spoorweg<br>U-Bahn | M ...... | Subway<br>Métro |
| Ondergrondse spoorweg in aanleg<br>U-Bahn in Bau | M ooooooo | Subway under construction<br>Métro en construction |
| Tram - Buslijn<br>Straßenbahn - Buslinie | ● ● | Tramway - Bus-route<br>Tramway - Ligne d'autobus |
| Autoveer - Veerpont<br>Autofähre - Personenfähre | | Car ferry - Passenger ferry<br>Bac pour automobiles - Bac pour piétonnes |
| Aanlegplaats - Sluis<br>Anlegestelle - Schleuse | ⚓    ◁ | Landing stage - Lock<br>Embarcadère - Écluse |
| Bezienswaardige kerk - Kerk<br>Sehenswerte Kirche - Kirche | ⊞    ⊞ | Church of interest - Church<br>Église remarquable - Église |
| Synagoge - Moskee<br>Synagoge - Moschee | ✡    ☾ | Synagogue - Mosque<br>Synagogue - Mosquée |
| Monument - Politiebureau<br>Denkmal - Polizeistation | ᛘ    ● | Monument - Police station<br>Monument - Poste de police |
| Postkantoor<br>Postamt | ✆ | Post office<br>Bureau de poste |
| Ziekenhuis - Jeugdherberg<br>Krankenhaus - Jugendherberge | ⊕    ▲ | Hospital - Youth hostel<br>Hôpital - Auberge de jeunesse |
| Vliegveldbus - Kampeerterrein<br>Flughafenbus - Campingplatz | B    ⋀ | Airport bus - Camping site<br>Bus d'aéroport - Terrain de camping |
| Windmolen<br>Windmühle | ⊼ | Windmill<br>Moulin à vent |
| Bebouwing - Openbaar gebouw<br>Bebaute Fläche - Öffentliches Gebäude | | Built-up area - Public building<br>Zone bâtie - Bâtiment public |
| Industrieterrein - Park, bos<br>Industriegelände - Park, Wald | | Industrial area - Park, forest<br>Zone industrielle - Parc, bois |
| MARCO POLO Avontuurlijke Route 1<br>MARCO POLO Erlebnistour 1 | | MARCO POLO Discovery Tour 1<br>MARCO POLO Tour d'aventure 1 |
| MARCO POLO Avontuurlijke Routes<br>MARCO POLO Erlebnistouren | | MARCO POLO Discovery Tours<br>MARCO POLO Tours d'aventure |
| MARCO POLO Highlight | ★1 | MARCO POLO Highlight |

# INDEX

This index lists all sights and excursion destinations featured in this guide, plus the names of some important terms, streets and squares. Numbers in bold indicate main entry.

# WRITE TO US

e-mail: info@marcopologuides.co.uk

Did you have a great holiday?
Is there something on your mind?
Whatever it is, let us know!
Whether you want to praise, alert us
to errors or give us a personal tip –
MARCO POLO would be pleased to
hear from you.
We do everything we can to provide
the very latest information for your trip.

Nevertheless, despite all of our authors'
thorough research, errors can creep
in. MARCO POLO does not accept any
liability for this. Please contact us by
e-mail or post.

MARCO POLO Travel Publishing Ltd
Pinewood, Chineham Business Park
Crockford Lane, Chineham
Basingstoke, Hampshire RG24 8AL
United Kingdom

### PICTURE CREDITS

Cover photograph: Amsterdam, canal with houseboats (Getty Images: F. Lemmens)
Photographs: Marit Beemster (18 top); DuMont Bildarchiv: Kiedrowski (8, 43), T. Linkel (7, 18 bottom); DUS architects (18 centre); R. Freyer (72, 108/109); Getty Images: I. Dobrolyubova (112), franckreporter (3), F. Lemmens (1), maydays (34), svariophoto (2), G. Tsafos (flap left, 5), S. Winter (56/57); Getty Images/Digital Vision (112/113); Getty Images/Image Source (9, 114 bottom); huber-images: A. Armellin (30, 41, 94/95), M. Rellini (38, 126/127); Laif: M. Gonzalez (47, 68/69, 78, 81, 89), M. Jäger (19 bottom), T. Linkel (flap right, 11, 14, 16/17, 26/27, 9, 114 top); Laif/Arcaid: A. Secci (52/53); Laif/hemis.fr: Ludovic/Maisant (86), L. Maisant (66); Laif/Hollandse Hoogte: Burgler (111), C. de Kruijf (51), Engbers (23), Riel (76/77, 115); Laif/Le Figaro Magazine: S. Gladieu (61); Laif/REA: F. Beloncle (84/85); Look: R. Mirau (42), M. Zegers (70); Look/SagaPhoto: (101), Forget (75, 83); Look/Travelstock44 (91); mauritius images/age: (104), A. Leiva (33); mauritius images/Alamy: (10, 60 right, 63, 65), L. Forster (60 left), T. Graham (6), The Foto Factory (93); mauritius images/imagebroker: Gabriel (48), Mateo (20/21); mauritius images/robertharding: J. Langley (4 top, 12/13); mauritius images/Westend61: R. Bellevue (19 top), D. Santiago Garcia (4 bottom, 54/55); picture-alliance/EPA: F. Damman (113), R. De Waal (24), K. Van Veel (110/111); vario images/Johnér Bildbyrå (110); Visum: E. van der Marel (45, 58)

9th Edition – fully revised and updated 2018
Worldwide Distribution: Marco Polo Travel Publishing Ltd, Pinewood, Chineham Business Park,
Crockford Lane, Basingstoke, Hampshire RG24 8AL, United Kingdom. Email: sales@marcopolouk.com
© MAIRDUMONT GmbH & Co. KG, Ostfildern
Chief editor: Marion Zorn
Author: Anneke Bokern; Editor: Christina Sothmann
Programme supervision: Stephan Dürr, Lucas Forst-Gill, Susanne Heimburger, Nikolai Michaelis, Martin Silbermann, Kristin Wittemann
Picture editors: Gabriele Forst, Anja Schlatterer; What's hot: wunder media, Munich
Cartography street atlas & pull-out map: © MAIRDUMONT, Ostfildern
Design cover, p. 1, cover pull-out map: Karl Anders – Büro für Visual Stories, Hamburg; interior design: milchhof:atelier, Berlin; design p. 2/3, Discovery Tours: Susan Chaaban Dipl.-Des. (FH)
Translated from German by John Sykes, Cologne; Jennifer Walcoff Neuheiser, Tübingen
Prepress: writehouse, Cologne; InterMedia, Ratingen
Phrase book in cooperation with Ernst Klett Sprachen GmbH, Stuttgart,
Editorial by Pons Wörterbücher

MIX
Paper from
responsible sources
FSC® C124385
www.fsc.org

# DOS & DON'TS! ✋

**Some things are best avoided in Amsterdam**

## DON'T ASSUME EVERYONE SPEAKS ENGLISH

The Dutch are fantastically good linguists. Most people you meet in tourist places will readily communicate in English, many of them fluently, and they don't expect foreigners to master their own language. Nevertheless, it often pays dividends to at least learn a few basics like "thank you", "good morning" and "please".

## DO VENTURE OUTSIDE THE CITY CENTRE

Many visitors to Amsterdam never manage to leave the axis between the Wallen, the canal ring and Museumplein, no matter how long they stay. Granted, the historic city centre is quite lovely and most of Amsterdam's main sightseeing attractions are located within these rings. But, Amsterdam has much more to offer. Hop aboard the ferry to Noord, head out for dinner at one of the many new and hip restaurants in Oost, or check out the little shops in De Pijp. If you really want to get to know the city, you have to take in its multicultural, alternative, modern, and lesser known sides. Plus, many of the hotels, cafés, and restaurants in these districts are more affordable than in the heart of the city centre. A jaunt across Stadhouderskade or the IJ is well worth the effort!

## DON'T DRIVE INTO THE CENTRE

It is quite a hassle to drive in Amsterdam's city centre. The streets are narrow, cyclists race past left and right, lorries clog the roads, and a place to park is virtually impossible to find. Do yourself a favour and park the car at a Park + Ride lot on the edge of the city or just leave your car at home. Most locals do the same; only 1 in 4 Amsterdammers even owns a car. By contrast, 35 per cent use a bike to get around town, whilst another 20 per cent prefer to walk. So opt for a pleasant stroll along the canals, hop on a tram or rent a bike to get around town. You'll be glad you did.

## DON'T ONLY DRINK HEINEKEN

Heineken, Amstel, and Grolsch are the Dutch beer brands that most people know, and they are available all over the world. That's why you should try something else when you're in Amsterdam itself. The city is home to a few microbreweries that produce much more interesting beers with a local touch, and you won't find them at home or elsewhere in the Netherlands. Have you ever heard of the breweries called *Oedipus*, *'t IJ*, or *'t Arendsnest*? That's just the point. Many of these breweries offer unusual craft beers, some of which are also organic. The selection ranges in style from double IPAs to strong Bock beers and seasonal specialities.